What Are They Saying About Masculine Spirituality?

David C. James, Ph.D.

PAULIST PRESS
New York/Mahwah, N.J.

Library of Congress Cataloging-in-Publication Data

James, David C., 1955-
   What are they saying about masculine spirituality? / David C. James.
      p.   cm.
   Includes bibliographical references.
   ISBN 0-8091-3632-5 (alk. paper)
   1. Men (Christian theology) 2. Men—Religious Life. 3. Spirituality—Catholic Church. 4. Catholic Church—Doctrines. I. Title.
BT703.5.J36   1996   95-36345
248′.081—dc20   CIP

Published by Paulist Press
997 Macarthur Boulevard
Mahwah, New Jersey 07430

Printed and bound in the
United States of America

Contents

Introduction

The battle of the spiritual man is always with himself. Today we are seeing the sad results of our failure to prepare men for this battle. When great religion no longer teaches and defines our deepest soul, we face life unprepared for the trials that will surely come our way. The effects are all around us: legitimated and even glorified violence, compulsive addiction, breakdown of foundational relationships, projection of shame and blame, and a common inability to believe in ourselves, others and life in general.

It seems that we do not have the time or the skill to learn the great patterns for ourselves. They are learned over generations and passed down through what first seem like empty aphorisms, rituals, and commandments. From current replacements such as "What goes around comes around" to classing proclamations of "Christ has died, Christ has risen, Christ will come again," the soul must imbibe the truths that it will not learn or is unable to learn by logic, computer or mere intelligence. We Christians call it divine revelation; Jews call it Torah and Talmud; most native peoples searched for such truth in myths, taboos, and consistently repeated feasts and ceremonies. Often, even mostly operating on a subliminal and unconscious level, great religion grounds, names, and liberates us for great truth. For God.

For a dozen different reasons many people, men and women, are unable or unwilling to hear these great truths through the mediation of western religious institutions. The language of personal trust, divine union, and living presence is not even considered because the first longings are untapped or even unrecognized. For many we have to go back to those primordial images and words in the presence of which we first opened our eyes to God: mother love, nature, silence, religious ceremony that "worked," childhood pictures that evoked awe, our first true love, the negative experiences of fear, betrayal, abandonment, and grief. Masculine and feminine spirituality are both trying to rebuild the gender foundations so that a grounded church can rise again.

Like all good teachers, David James is giving us something more than mere concepts that we can merely agree or disagree about. He is opening up perspectives, providing vision, images and stories that allow us to rediscover the great truths for ourselves. Hopefully we can see it is the same truth that our ancestors were talking about, and that the church is desperately trying to proclaim. It is called tradition and along with scripture is one of the two "fonts" of good theology. I think this book is leading us back to both of these fonts where we can drink long and deep. David is also giving us some suggestions for process and containment where men can grieve, rant, and sit in the belly of the whale without needing someone to blame or attack. I think that is precisely the mystery of church. Finally it leads to shared contentment and even rejoicing.

In this post-modern era we need a spirituality which appreciates the non-rational cyclic meanings instead of mere linear progress, the importance of the dark side of our spiritual education, which is also the importance of the outcast, the poor, and the failure in our lives. We need to move away from the false individualism of modernism back to social connectedness, to communal religion that is accountable for what it says it believes. I think David's book is calmly but clearly aiming us back—yet forward—to such foundations. Modern world views separated religion and science, the feminime from the masculine. Women have rightly become mistrustful of technology and power; men have unfortunately become mistrustful of religion and spirituality. Externalization and inner-ness can no longer operate on different tracks. We need a language and an experience that connect rather than react. We need some fundamental teaching that begins with union and aims toward fur-ther union. That will only come from great religion.

Our religious leaders have largely found themselves incapable of writing a pastoral letter on women, but it has never even occurred to them to write one on men. We seem to have resigned ourselves to church meetings where men are largely absent, to church ministry that is mainly done by women but overseen by a clerical caste, to an often soft devotionalism that attracts only a specific male clientele. Usually the men who do become involved in church are subservient types and not the risk takers, leaders, and missionary personalities that attract other men. This is increasingly apparent in minority neighborhoods of the world where the men with religious desire invariably move toward evangelical churches and community service projects. We cannot continue to lose such men under a false banner of orthodoxy when it is usually an issue of control. It must be significant that Jesus chose working men, independent types, even a Zealot and a would-be betrayer to get this whole thing started. We are choos-ing our religious leaders from an increasingly narrow category. We can do much better.

Books like this give me hope. Not only is it written by a man who is willing to "hang in there," and trust the Spirit, but David enthusiastically invites other men to join him on the great adven-ture that is the search for God. Let's go!

Richard Rohr, O.F.M.

Foreword

A phenomenon known as the "men's movement" is emerging as a distinct process in the evolution of personal and social consciousness. This process of definition and redefinition is underway with intensity. Whether in gatherings or in solitary reflection, there is a hunger on the part of men to understand the potential of their masculine spirit. Questions of identification, empowerment, connection, development and relationship take on greater importance as men seek new paradigms for masculine living. The scope of men's deliberation is not limited to issues related to personal gain, but rather embraces communitarian, familial and societal renovation. In other words, men are interested in appropriate uses of masculine power to contribute to the advancement of humankind.

Definitions and paradigms that were heretofore accepted as the norm to judge "masculine" behavior and thinking are recognized as being outdated and, in some instances, harmful to both men and women. Patriarchy, that is, *the rule of the fathers*, has been the source of critical reflection for some time in gender studies. Feminists have long assailed both the damaging historical consequences of patriarchy as well as its current threat to authentic human coexistence. Men's studies are now offering discriminating reflections on the effects of patriarchy upon the personal/psychological development and socialization of young men.

As is true with any ground-breaking field of study, the "men's movement" has both its critics and its supporters. Many feminists are wary of a movement that could potentially limit if not obviate the gains that women have made over the past twenty-five years. Many would argue that men have always been "on the top of the pile," and, as such, don't need any further advantage. Such critiques are not always accurate or fair. A new term, "misandry," or the prejudice against the masculine, has been added to the lexicon of gender studies. At times there seems to be an "open season" on anything that touches the masculine in academic or political circles. The "men's movement" seeks to address such inaccurate and sometimes prejudicial philosophies with an honest critique of the abuses of patriarchy, and yet offer a compelling witness to the beneficence of masculine power. As will be demonstrated in this book, the "men's movement" can be viewed as a complementary movement of grace to encourage more authentic and life-giving connections between men and women.

Feminists are not the only critics of the "men's movement." The challenge of the "men's movement" to commonly held cultural assumptions about "manliness" engages men in a dialogue about their very existence. As such, there is little neutral exchange on this topic. Often the popular caricature of the "men's movement" is that of a gathering of neurotic young executives trying to overcome their angst and greed in a native American sweat lodge. The "sensitive new-age guy" is a stereotypical image often offered by those who mistake serious masculine reflection for egocentric introspection. To address these criticisms, the "men's movement" seeks to identify the connection between introspection and life-giving action. A common theme emerging in men's reflections is that to be truly effective, the masculine spirit must be connected to the depths of the soul, while actively participating in the core issues of the day.

One of the major components of the "men's movement" is the study of masculine spirituality. Authors in this discipline point to the necessity of a spirituality which is both distinctively masculine, and yet not anti-feminine. Just as an authentic feminist spirituality empowers women to access the fullest depths of their souls and connect them to the divine, so too does authentic masculine spirituality.

So this leads to the question: What does an authentic spirituality for men look like? Or perhaps more to the point, how will a spirituality that is centered in masculine imagery allow men access to the divine, or, as one author calls it, the God-path? In some regards, that is the purpose of this book. The intent is to review the different ways that men, and to some degree women, are thinking about the relationship between God and man.[1]

By way of introduction, it appears that a masculine spirituality has symbiotic relationships with a number of disciplines. Depth psychology, somatic disciplines, mytho-poetic literature, anthropology and religious sources all inform masculine spirituality. As is the case with other emerging spiritual practices, much of the work in this field is being done by men "in the trenches." These men, meeting in lodges, circles, retreats, and various encounter groups, are unsatisfied with traditional pieties and religious formulas. They talk, study the ancient gods of men, drum as a group, and seek soul images that resonate within and call them to their depths. In some regards it is certainly a case of reflection following praxis. So, while there are common themes and movements taking shape in this endeavor, much of the exciting work has yet be done. It is also worth noting that while the "men's movement" is in the infancy of its development, the development of masculine spirituality is yet in its genesis stage. Accordingly, Christian reflections upon the masculine spirit are barely underway.

Since this work will attempt to introduce and synthesize the topic of masculine spirituality, I will address the following five questions: (1) What is the mythology of masculine spirituality?

---

1. Throughout this work, "man" will be used in the specific sense, while "human" or "humankind" will refer to both men and women.

This will be an overview of the basic premises of masculine spirituality. (2) How crucial is it for masculine spirituality that God be male? This discussion will focus on the continued debate on gender roles for God, but, more specifically, will address the role that male imagery places in the religious imagination of man. (3) What are the soul images of a man? This will be an attempt to understand the relationship of the inner movement of a man to archetypal patterns of king, warrior, magician, and lover. These archetypes, a reflection of the influence of depth psychology, are becoming commonly identified as the patterns of relationship that operate within the psyche of a man. This chapter also addresses the value of mythological reflection for men as they seek to understand the common patterns of masculine development. (4) How does masculine spirituality integrate a man? This discussion will focus on the relationship between a man's body, soul and spirit, and the possibility offered by masculine spirituality to effect such an integration. (5) Where is the community of a man? This will examine the value of a communally-based masculine spirituality.

I hope that this book stimulates the reader's interest in masculine spirituality. Its value is that it introduces the reader to a variety of authors involved in various conversations about masculine spirituality. It is an exciting time to be part of these conversations, and if after reading this work you are stimulated to explore for yourself the unfolding richness of masculine spirituality, then I've accomplished the task I set before me.

A number of people have been part of my developing spirituality, so to them go my most profound thanks.

- To my parents Don and JoAnne James.
- To Rich Gula, S.S. for his proofreading and editorial assistance.
- To Richard Rohr, O.F.M. for his contributions and writing the "Introduction" to this book.
- To James Clarke, for his insights, proofreading and suggestions.

- To Doug Fisher at Paulist Press for his encouragement.
- To Rod Whitacre and Steve Smith of the Trinity Episcopal School for Ministry.
- To St. Patrick's Seminary, Menlo Park—especially Gerald D. Coleman, S.S.
- To Edd Anthony, O.F.M., and the Franciscan Canticle for support in men's work.
- To Skip Day, Jack Barker, Warren Nyback, Leo Wisnewski, R. Francis Stevenson, Mark Fields, Steve Meriwether, Joe Schwab, O.F.M.—good friends all.
- To Patrick Callahan for encouraging me through my Ph.D.
- To Michael Magallon for teaching me about courage in difficult circumstances.
- To Audrey Magallon, and my daughters Erin and Jessica who are teaching me how to love the feminine.

Finally, this book is dedicated to my nephew Nathan VanNote. His future is bright and filled with promise. I hope the work of this generation of men will give him hope for the future.

1
The Mythology
of Masculine Spirituality

Masculine spirituality, that is, a spirituality intentionally grounded in the symbols, stories and reflections of men, is likely to be misunderstood. Masculine spirituality speaks to and for men as they journey on the God-path toward wholeness and individuation. But to address issues specifically related to men is somehow to invite criticism. In this day and age, there is a great deal of suspicion surrounding anything that touches men and spirituality.

Accepted notions of "manliness" in the late twentieth century are being transformed in the light of both popular and serious reflection. A generation ago, gender roles were more established than today. A man "knew" his place as the breadwinner and *paterfamilias*. He was characterized by assertiveness, competence, individuality, strength and responsibility. Today conflicted images of masculinity have emerged. The cultural icon of masculine identity—the self-sufficient, swaggering, movie action hero—is compelling to some segments of society and repelling to others. To counter this, a new wave of "sensitive" and yet "virile" male movie stars have captured the hearts of both men and women. This might be pointing to a change in the consciousness of society. In the same way, while the rough and tumble of professional sports still holds a fascinating grip over men in our culture, other forms of sacrificial endeavor such as the arts, sciences and healthy social action are becoming ever more accepted as expressions of a healthy masculinity.

Having said this, however, it is important to note that with the evolution of the masculine identity and the ascendence of feminist influences in society, there is more than a little misandrist, or anti-masculine opinion evidenced in both the popular culture and the academic world. From the critical spirit of television talk shows to some feminist literature, a myriad of derisive masculine images have flooded our collective awareness. These suggest that being a man is, for the first time, more of a deficit than a benefit.[1]

In the ever broadening world of theological reflection, there are some feminist critiques of the development of a masculine based spirituality. Their argument is that men have always experienced power and privilege on the world stage, and that male dominance has resulted in destruction, pollution and death. Whether or not it is because men are biologically inferior as some feminists perceive them,[2] men are caricatured in our culture as being stupid and likely to cause harm.[3] According to this paradigm, any spiritual reflection that explores masculine ways of thinking about the relationship between God and a man is bound to be ultimately harmful. This assumption suggests that women have everything to fear and nothing to gain from men developing a strong spiritual life. It also demonstrates the myopic tendencies of feminist critics. While men have been responsible for horrible atrocities and tragedies, so too have they been responsible for many of the greatest advances of humankind.[4] In light of feminist critiques, an honest assessment of the contributions of men is essential to develop an authentic sense of the potentialities and liabilities of men. Masculine spirituality recognizes the harmful effects of patriarchy on both men and women and it appreciates the gains made by women's spirituality.[5]

Masculine spirituality recognizes that the call to live as a man on the God-path is a responsibility that can best be undertaken apart from the influence of women. As Philip Culbertson notes:

The women's movement is light-years ahead of the men's movement, and much that has been achieved by feminism has happened because women went away from men to work through their issues. The time has now come for men to go away from women to do our own homework within the intentional community of sensitive men. Until we have sorted through a number of critical same-sex identity issues, we are not ready to build a new future of men and women together. We must build on sameness before we are ready to build on differences.[6]

This perception is based, at least in part, on the anthropological evidence of initiatory rites where boys are removed from the "world of women" and brought to manhood by ritualistic association with men.[7] Some developmental psychologists also argue for the necessity of a man's individuation away from the influences and psychic controls of the feminine to ensure a healthy sense of interdependence.[8] It is this vision of interdependence that masculine spirituality seeks to explore and incarnate. Masculine spirituality is not concerned with living in a world without women, or living in a world where women are subordinate to men. Rather it wants men to exist as co-creators with women in healthy relationships with the rest of creation. While a discussion of masculine individuation will take place in Chapter 3, let it suffice to say that the goal of developing a vibrant masculine spirit is to live fully as men in relationship with women who are experiencing their own fullness, vitality and vision.

The challenge, therefore, for masculine spirituality is to continue to unfold the richness of its emerging tradition in spite of unfair criticism, and yet access as widely as possible the movements within feminist and other theologies that lend themselves to healthy dialogue and growth.[9] One of the particular challenges faced by those involved in developing masculine spirituality is coming to a consensus as to the appropriate definition of what it means to be "masculine." Later in this chapter I will show that there is an ongoing debate about the nature of masculinity. One end of the spectrum argues that a "wild man" image most effectively connotes what it means to be masculine, while at the other end masculinity is defined by a man's ability to be "sensitive." Just as feminist theologians are involved in clarifying definition and paradigm, so too are those who are reflecting on masculine spirituality. This is bound to produce both controversy and a rich harvest of insight.

Movements in the Symphony of Masculine Spirituality

Masculine spirituality, like all developing theologies, can best be characterized, not so much as a complete system with concrete principles and axioms, but as a grand symphony still being written. Each movement of the symphony has its own characteristic components, and yet there is an underlying melody that provides unity to the work. This chapter will examine the movements of masculine spirituality in an attempt to discover the grand and glorious melody sounding throughout.[10] In other words, the arena of men and their capacity for healthy relationships will be explored. First, I will review the dynamic of a man's relationship with his mother and father to see how they affect his ability to relate to himself and others. Then I will examine a model of masculine development that many men find helpful on their quest to wholeness. Finally, I will explore the question, "What does a real man look like?" This will be a review of two authors who hold dissimilar views as to the direction of masculine development.

Men and Relationships

Relationships are what makes life work. The connection that relationships both provide and demand is the essential avenue for existence. All relationships, be they professional, social, familial, religious, or cultural, entail a level of interaction between the participants. For one to relate to another requires a measure of ability and desire. Relationships for men, and those who live with them, are often a source of frustration and contention. Men are accused of being "distant" and "aloof." Generally the only emotions that men feel free to display are those related to sexual expression and anger.

There is a great deal of support for these accusations. For example, almost without exception, those who write on men's issues point to the "psychic numbing" of men. "Psychic numbing" connotes a loss of emotional and physical awareness which limits a man's emotional and psychic capacity. As a result, these men live Thoreau's "lives of quiet desperation," out of touch with their bodies, unable to relate to others, and susceptible to a host of addictions and compulsions.[11] The end result of these emotional deficits is that men feel lonely, disconnected and unable to enter into meaningful relationships.[12]

The inability to form authentic relationships influences the very essence of a man's God-path. Any number of definitions of spirituality speak to the need for spirituality to be connected to relationships.[13] For spirituality to be authentic, it must be united to a relationship not only with "the Other" but also with "others." Since the focus of the Christian moral message is unconditional love of others, it demands much of all relationships. Men must be able to relate and love as wholeheartedly and honestly as possible. Sadly, this isn't the case for many men today.

The Woman and the Son

One of the chief reasons for the inability of twentieth century man to participate in healthy relationships is the nature of the socialization he has received. The process of raising a child to adulthood is accomplished ideally by both father and mother. As such, each has a definitive role to play. By and large, the way that boys are nurtured and raised, by both mother and father, is considerably different than girls. While there is value to the different ways that fathers and mothers express their love, it has been suggested that contemporary methods of raising boys by both genders are deficient.

Aaron Kipnis reports on the studies of the relationship between a mother and her infant son which show that boys are not held as much as girls, and that boys are left alone in their cribs more often than girls.[14] When held by their mothers, boys are more likely to be positioned so that they face away, whereas girls are held in a manner where they are drawn into the body of their mother. Boys are usually weaned from the mother much earlier than girls, and this enhances their growing sense of separation. As the boys grow older, their sense of estrangement from their mother continues. Boys are not spoken to as much as girls are, and when they are spoken to, it is not age appropriate. Rather boys are expected to communicate at a more complex level than girls, and this puts a strain on the cognitive development of boys.[15] The behavioral sciences have demonstrated that there are tragic consequences as a result of the separation between mother and son.[16] Psychologically, many of a man's feminine characteristics should have been developed through a healthy interaction with his mother. More often than not, however, social conditioning keeps mother and son apart, and this tends to make the feminine world both fascinating and threatening at the same time.[17]

The health of the mother-son relationship has several implications for the development of an authentic masculine spirituality. Foremost of these is that the lack of effective maternal socialization contributes to an anti-feminine bias in the developing boy. If a boy both loves and hates the feminine, then he enters adulthood conflicted. Women are objects to be used and not people to relate to. Girlfriends, wives, work associates, and ultimately daughters become "things" that exist to make the man happy, rather than being partners in the experience of life. Seminary personnel speak about the hatred of the feminine that is displayed by many in formation programs.[18] Celibacy is often used by seminarians as an escape from the feminine, but this in turn leads to the degradation of their female colleagues and parishioners. As one female seminary faculty member commented to her colleagues, "I'm either a mother, a lover, or a sister to every guy in this house." The man who is either afraid of women or obsessed with them is unable to live an authentic Christian life, because he is incapable of respectful and healthy interactions necessary for inter-dependent relationships with them.

Second, the man with a distorted view of the feminine has an incomplete view of God. Contrary to much of the mythology of the ancient world, classic Christian theology teaches that God is neither male nor female, but fully both. Chapter 2 will show that it is necessary for a man to connect with masculine images of God, as they are the ones most apt to energize his relationship with the divine.[19] At this point, however, it is important to note that there is more to God than the masculine gender. So when a man is alienated from the feminine world, he has distanced himself from an essential part of his relationship with God. Additionally, when a man is wary of the feminine, he is bound to restrict his access to the "nurturing" characteristics of God, which he automatically equates with femininity.[20] The "masculinization" of God by patriarchy will be demonstrated in greater depth in Chapter 2.

Finally, a man who has an underdeveloped appreciation of the feminine is most likely going to have difficulty with intimacy, his own body and sexuality. The mother is the first person to "initiate" the infant boy into a relationship of intimacy, usually at the breast. If the prevailing social notions of child rearing prevail, and the boy is weaned from the breast earlier than girls, he develops an innate sense that intimate connections with mother are somehow wrong, even "naughty." Developmental psychology has demonstrated that men's inability to be intimate is born in such moments. The guilt associated with sexuality is often conveyed in the relationship between mother and son. It appears that in their roles as the primary caretaker of children in our society, mothers have a great influence on the development of their sons' ability to integrate sexual aspects of their nature which lead to healthy intimacy.[21]

The ability to be intimate touches the very essence of masculine spirituality. Men are incarnated into body with a whole range of emotions, feelings and inter-relationships which connect them to God. If a man feels guilty about intimacy and dissociated from his body, then he will be alienated from the very capacities that allow him to relate to others. Any short-circuiting of a man's capacity for intimacy leads to a distortion of his relationship with God. As will be demonstrated in Chapter 3, a restoration of man's ability to appreciate his relationship with the feminine will lead to healing his sexuality, and thus open another avenue of his awareness of God.

Fathers and Sons

While the separation from the mother is devastating to a boy, those who study men submit that the loss of a father's love and energy is even more destructive. Key to the authentic development of a boy's masculine identity is the transmission of life energy from his father. As noted above, a boy's mother is the first person from whom he will learn intimacy and connection. Ideally, his father will be the first to teach him about separation, identification, and differentiation.

Behavioral scientists have produced a wealth of resources to validate the notion that the father holds a key role in the development of his son. Without a father's loving presence, the boy begins to question his essential value. But with paternal love and nurturance, a boy experiences the foundations necessary for a healthy masculine sense of self-worth. As Arnold notes:

> Every boy needs to relate to a father who will give him a permanent sense of security, a psychic safe-place of sureness and strength that tells him that he belongs, that he is wanted, and that he will make it with a little work. Every boy needs to know that his father is on his side, pulling for him, giving him paternal energy so that whatever he does, he knows he can succeed. If the boy does not receive such assurance from his father, he cannot recreate a firm psychic center within himself, and he is left with a terrible lack of self-esteem and confidence.[22]

One of the tragic realities of the late twentieth century is that there is no more disconnected relationship than that of the father and son. Among the observers of masculine culture there is consensus that what should be the closest of relationships has become, in fact, the most distant.[23] Some note that in this generation, fathers work long hours away from the home. As a result, they have little time or inclination to be involved in rearing their sons. Others suggest that fathers, themselves the product of a deficit in masculine rearing practices, are ill equipped to participate in the raising of a son. Regardless of the reason for his absence, the common conclusion is that the more time that a father spends away from home and family, the greater is the likelihood that he will not be able to relate, mirror and affirm when he is present. Where the father was once the non-maternal center of a boy's universe, he is now more likely to be viewed as a distant and unapproachable figure with little investment in his child. Consequently, boys are raised by their mothers, and the resulting loss is inestimable. The "Father Wound" or "Father Hunger" in many men is profound as they yearn for the masculine comfort, support and challenge that a father should provide.[24]

Children are unable psychologically to discriminate when it comes to the actions of parents. So when a father absents himself either physically or psychologically, the son believes that he is deficient in some profound way. The results of the "Father Wound" are devastating. Confusion about sexual identity, a distorted sense of self-esteem, repression of aggressive impulses, diminished ambition, learning problems, contempt of moral values or responsibility, and a greater propensity toward drug and alcohol abuse are the hallmarks of the abandoned son.[25] Rebellion is often a characteristic pattern in the lives of boys who grow up without a father's energy and guidance. Authority figures find themselves the target of a young man's father-anger. As a result, confrontation and/or passive-aggressive behavior will be manifested, since the angry young man doesn't possess either the capacity or the skills for honest interaction.

Psychologists argue that the drive for a father's love is so strong that if a young man is abandoned either geographically or emotionally by his father, he will go on a quest to find a surrogate father. Perhaps this surrogate will be an authority figure, a celebrity, an athlete, or a successful executive. Regardless of the profession, the surrogate will be someone who can mirror the boy, affirm him and tell him in any number of ways that he is valuable. This need for masculine acceptance takes a destructive turn when the young man associates with a group such as a criminal gang. Countless numbers of boys interviewed have indicated that in their "gang" they receive support, affirmation and acceptance in a way that they never have before. As will be demonstrated in Chapter 5, some writers suggest that the impulse to gather as a "tribe" is rooted in archetypal yearnings of men, and that gangs are a deadly derivation of a basic masculine need for fellowship and masculine cooperative endeavor.

There are several implications for men as it relates to the "Father Wound" and developing a masculine spirituality. Since it appears that a father's love is essential to healthy personality development, the first implication is that there are numbers of men walking about without a positive sense of personal identity. The image of the "macho man" is an example of the definitive loss of a man's center. Those men whose personal development is distorted are unable to connect with their most resourceful self, and they are at a loss to interact honestly or with integrity.

This loss of the center is manifest in many ways. Compulsive behaviors such as substance addictions, overwork, and eating disorders are symptomatic of the loss of one's center. Having never been grounded in a masculine psychology that is secure and centered, the necessary sense of balance in a man's life is thrown off. This is most typically apparent in a man's inability to relate to his own emotions. Characteristically, men have been taught to repress most expressions of their emotions with the exception of the "classic" male emotions of lust and anger. As a result, the wide range of emotions necessary for authentic personal existence are repressed. This takes its toll on a man's psycho-physiological sense of well-being. Additionally, when the full range of emotions are repressed, the ability to understand one's own feelings is limited. This in turn limits one's ability to relate to others. It has been suggested that the "shallow masculine," or the common masculine persona, handicaps a man's ability to relate to others. Men by virtue of their stunted personal development are unable to relate freely and fully to other men, and to women even less.

As noted above, chief among the relationships that suffer when a man has no sense of personal identity is his relationship with God. If a man doesn't feel connected to men or masculine emotions, it follows that he will have difficulty relating to that which is the source of his being, God. Masculine spirituality seeks to find paths that lead a man on a pilgrimage of presence both to himself and to God. This by necessity involves "inner work" that connects a man to his emotions and to relationships. Support groups, psychosynthesis, dreamwork, journal writing, guided imagery and meditative practices are offered so that men can learn to relate to all the facets of their personality. In doing so, they can appreciate the goodness of that which is male, including the maleness of God.

The Measure of a Man

The discussion about the development of masculine spirituality has been focused so far on the inter-relationship between a man and others. I have yet to examine the question of personal development for its own sake and the role that masculine spirituality plays in this regard. In other words, is there an ideal model of the spiritual man? The general consensus is that a "spiritual man" is one who, though of various personality types, is connected deeply to his sacred center and well on his way toward a maturing emotional and psycho-spiritual life. Evident in this type of balanced spirituality will be a sense of centeredness, awareness and authenticity. Two reflections will be offered to address this consideration. The first examines a model of masculine development and the second examines the debate in the men's movement that surrounds the sensitive male.

There is no debate among developmental theorists that human growth occurs in stages. Likewise, there is no serious debate that boys develop at a different pace than girls. Controversy arises when issues of genetics and environment are brought into the discussion. The most commonly accepted premise is that there is a balance between a person's genetic inheritance and the influence of one's environment on development. In this regard, masculine spirituality suggests that while a person's genetic structure and environment both play a crucial role, there is another factor to be included in the debate—that of divine presence and influence. This God-closeness doesn't necessarily negate the psychological schemas of development such as Freud's or Erickson's. What it amplifies is the connection between the personal and transcendent dimensions in the development of the man.

The Two Journeys

In their book *The Wildman's Journey*, Richard Rohr and Joseph Martos offer a model of divinely influenced masculine development. Under the title "The Two Journeys," the authors suggest that men develop along a common path. Using a mix of biblical imagery and archetypal psychology, the authors seek to illustrate that there are two journeys of personal development, influenced by culture, yet open to the transforming power of grace. They note that all men begin their path toward individuation in the stage they call "The Common Masculine." This stage is most typically identified as the "All American Man." Confidence, self-assurance, independence and resourcefulness are the hallmarks of this type of man. The authors identify him as the "self-made man" that men emulate and women adore.[26] The stage of the common masculine lacks vulnerability, sensitivity, receptiveness and intuition, and, as such, masculine spirituality recognizes the limitations of this period in a man's life. Given the cultural matrix of the United States, this type of man is often the norm for a boy's socialization. In other words, "everyone wants to be like him."

At this juncture the man makes a choice as to which path he will follow. If the cultural model of masculinity holds sway in his life, he will move from the common masculine to what Rohr/Martos call "the shallow masculine." In the shallow masculine, a man tends to be "the tough guy." Here he rejects any character traits that are perceived to be "weak" and exemplifies the "macho" and sexist attitudes prevalent in much of society today. Unfortunately, many men enter into the shallow masculine and remain there, since this is the only model of manliness they have. Any notion that men have a "sensitive side" is dismissed with scorn as being appropriate only for "sissies or homosexuals." Much of the critique of patriarchy finds its objections personified in the common and shallow masculine, as neither of these modes of masculine expression lends itself to collaboration or mutuality. Rather, others are objectified and seen as means for pleasure or contempt.

The alternate path for the man is the movement into "the common feminine." It is in this stage that he begins to understand and accept traits and drives within that have been suppressed or rejected. Empathy, intuition, receptiveness, tenderness and similar traits are more commonly associated with women, and yet they exist within a man as well. Rohr/Martos note that the first attempts at connection with the feminine occur in external relationships, with mothers, girlfriends, wives, etc. Next, however, the man must engage in a journey for which the common culture doesn't prepare him—namely, connection with authentic feminine energy within. The authors have labeled this stage of individuation as "The Journey of John the Beloved." This biblical imagery typifies a man who has accepted both his need for and his ability to be both feeling and expressive. Rohr/Martos suggest that if a man doesn't enter into the stage of the common feminine, he will remain in the grip of the shallow masculine. Further they indicate that if a man remains "stuck" in the common feminine, he runs the risk of descending into the stage of the "shallow feminine." As might be expected, the shallow feminine is that state where the typically masculine traits of focus, determination, self-confidence and inner authority are lacking. When a man is in the grip of the shallow feminine, he can be stereotypically portrayed as a "soft man," one so in touch with his feelings that he can't seem to escape them.

To counter this, Rohr/Martos point to the necessary next step of "The Journey of John the Baptist." Now acquainted with his "inner feminine," the man moves toward deeper psychic energies which will thrust him toward complete individuation.[27] In other words, he must walk away from the suppositions of the common masculine, into an exploration and acceptance of the feminine, and back toward the energies of the deep masculine as constitutive parts of his God-path. Independence, assertiveness, focus, and strength of character are all traits exhibited by men as they enter the deep masculine. There is even a sense of "wildness" about them as they tend to be less controlled by external norms and pressures than before.

As Rohr/Martos note, the deep masculine can be misunderstood as it can appear as a heightened version of the shallow masculine. Independence can be mistaken for arrogance, assertiveness for aggressiveness, focus for stubbornness, while strength of character can be misunderstood as domination. The crucial distinction is that a man cannot enter into his deep masculine energies unless he has already experienced a union with his feminine qualities. The developing feminine keeps a man empathetic and, as such, enables him to build, nurture and sustain himself as a co-creator with God.

The Sensitive Man

Writers differ on their understanding of the "sensitive man." Feminism rightly points out that men have often been so concerned with their own desires that they forget the value and presence of women. As men undertake the task of understanding and reconstructing their persona, questions about the "sensitive man" arise. I will only represent the positions of two authors from opposite ends of the spectrum to show the diversity of thinking in this regard.

In his book *The New Adam*, Philip Culbertson identifies the "masculine" in "masculine spirituality" as

> that which is appropriate to those males who have taken seriously the opportunity for their own liberation from gender stereotypes and have in the process begun to seek a new and more sensitive self-understanding in light of the feminist critique.[28]

Throughout this work, Culbertson idealizes the "sensitive man" as the goal for masculine development. By way of definition, a "sensitive man" is one who is aware of the full range of his emotions, comfortable with his body, able to relate in ways that are both linear (masculine) and circular (feminine), not afraid of women, and one who is willing to work with them as equal partners. He posits that there is a serious deficit in the common masculine personality as evidenced by the male obsession with virility, violence, emotional distancing, and the abuse of power.[29] An authentic masculine spirituality geared toward sensitivity must address twelve stumbling blocks:

- The identification of God as Father.
- The fear of the feminine.
- The domination by tradition-centered males of literature in theology and spiritual direction.
- The suppression of the broad range of human emotions.
- The valuation of self-sufficiency.
- The misunderstanding of reciprocal relationships.
- The insistence that "doing" is more manly than "being."
- The problem of men not knowing who they are when they aren't in charge.
- The heritage of body-soul dualism and the dismissal of body and sexuality.

- The need to control, the valuation of hierarchy, the fear of chaos and spontaneity.
- The assumption that incompleteness or an unpredictable result is a sign of failure.
- The preference for linearity over circularity, as conditioned by male anatomy and phallocentrism.[30]

Culbertson's thesis is similar to the thinking of most "post-feminist" theologians. A combination of humanist driven psychology and progressive theology informs this model of reflection. Key elements in this model are the reclaiming of repressed and/or suppressed psychic material, and the development of a counter-cultural image of sensitive masculinity in concert with other like-minded men.

Culbertson rejects the use of the popular paradigm of masculine development, the myth of "Iron John." The content of this myth and its implication for masculine spirituality will be developed in Chapter 3. To demonstrate his view of the sensitive man, Culbertson writes:

> We already know from the proper feminist critique of our inheritance what damage macho self-centeredness, conformity, and anti-intellectualism can produce. Instead of seeking the wild man within, sensitive men should seek to nurture and facilitate.[31]

To summarize, Culbertson appreciates the developments underway in the field of masculine spirituality. It is his dream to see men move toward "sensitivity" and engage post-feminist reflection from this perspective.

Patrick M. Arnold takes a different track in his development of the "ideal man" in his work, *Wildmen, Warriors and Kings: Masculine Spirituality and the Bible*. As a preface to his thought, he notes:

> ...the Christian Church along with much of Western culture is presently experiencing a transition from centuries of static mas-

culinity (patriarchy) to dynamic femininity (feminism); this movement is as inevitable as the tides and it cannot be stopped: the feminine is ascendent, the masculine in decline. This, too, shall pass....Masculinity itself is under attack, and not only in its negative shadow, but in its most positive qualities, too.[32]

In addition to scriptural scholarship, Arnold is influenced by socio-biology and archetypal psychology. As a result, he portrays the avenue for development of the mature masculine personality through a closer and more authentic identification with primal and physiological processes.

Biology influences everything men do, think and feel. Sometimes the results are unfortunate; more often, the outcome of all those hormones and chemicals coursing through the evolution designed male body is quite wonderful: hard work, intense play, strong protectiveness, outrageous humor, ardent passion, and feats of heroism. It is no shame for a man to realize his animal kinship with a stag or a bull or a rooster....[33]

Arnold suggests that masculine drives such as competitiveness, independence and autonomy, vulnerability and responsibility are rooted in psychological patterns not unique to men, but common to them. The direction of his work points to the danger of the "feminization" of men. He argues that men are created "by design" in the image of the "wildman" that Culbertson rejects. A major portion of his work is dedicated to trying to embody his sense of authentic masculinity in the images of Old Testament patriarchs, prophets, warriors, magicians, kings, healers and tricksters.

For Arnold, men are different from women and they should learn to appreciate and develop that difference. Arnold envisions the integration of the "anima" as an important part of the development of the masculine soul. To Arnold, a man must develop the ability to be connected to his emotions. This will come as he proceeds through four "moments" in his spiritual journey. The first stage of the *static feminine* represents the beginning place for each man. This stage connects a man to the elemental center of his psychic world. From this place of maternal connection the man is called to move through the stage of the *dynamic masculine* where separation and differentiation away from the static feminine occur. In this stage "the first thrusts of masculinity" are experienced and the young man connects with the outside world as "man." The *static masculine* is the next stage where "heroic masculine dynamism" is established as the man "settles down, consolidates and creates institutions and maintains them against the vicissitudes of time (conservatism)."[34] The final stage of a man's journey is that of the *dynamic feminine*. It is in this stage that the man develops his sense of depth and connects with inner wisdom, beauty and art. So Arnold sees the absolute necessity for a man to be connected with his depths, his feelings and his body. However, the sense of direction that a man goes with his energies could be seen in a different light than Culbertson's.

As with virtually all of the writings in masculine spirituality, both authors emphasize the importance of men assembling together for support and guidance. While Culbertson sees men striving together to become more sensitive, Arnold calls men to unite to discover ways of relating that are rooted in hearty masculine challenge and support. Arnold holds that, given the lack of authentic fathering most boys suffer from, the ideal would be for a "community of men" to develop life-giving and power-producing rites whereby the boy "becomes a man."[35] He offers the following ways that young men might be introduced into the life of spirit:

- Initiation rites
- Missionary outreach
- Pilgrimage
- Masculine-based liturgy and preaching
- Masculine prayer and devotions
- Men's discussion and support groups
- Church reforms away from its dominant feminist culture

This brief contrast demonstrates that Culbertson and Arnold recognize the same problem, the lack of an authentic masculine soul and its devastating impact upon both men and women. At this point, however, they diverge. Culbertson seems to shy away from that which Arnold advocates. Culbertson calls for "sensitive men" to emerge in society, whereas Arnold calls for men possessed of a vibrant masculine spirit to return to the wisdom of their archetypal heritage and potential. Culbertson declares the necessity for men to develop images other than that of the "Father-God," while Arnold invites men to get in touch with the power of masculine images in worship. Culbertson is delighted with the increased "feminization" of the Christian church and Arnold denounces it.

When painting a picture using only two colors, one always runs the risk of unfair dichotomy and a lack of adequate blending. Such could be the case with the above analysis. Culbertson and Arnold recognize the deficit in the contemporary masculine persona, and argue for the development of the authentic masculine soul. Both call for this soul work to be done away from the influences of women. Both rejoice in the goodness of the male, and both are committed to eliminating any form of the abuse of women. From this common ground, however, these men take the movement of masculine spirituality in dramatically different directions, and their reflections offer insight and direction to the movement of men.

Summary

This chapter has been an introduction into the "mythology" or reflective understanding of the growth of masculine spirituality. After introductory comments as to the validity of and need for developing a vibrant masculine spirituality, I offered reflections on the quagmire of contemporary men's relationships. In an attempt to understand men's inability to form authentic relationships, I reviewed the relationship between a boy and his mother and its effect upon his psychological development. Then I scrutinized the relationship of father to son, to see how much of a man's self-image is either shaped or warped by the attention paid to it. I examined the Rohr/Martos model of masculine development in order to show one mythic path that men are using today. Finally, I offered a brief comparison of Culbertson and Arnold's position on the "sensitive man" to shed some light on the variety of thought about the direction of development of men in the writings of Christian masculine spirituality.

The evolution of masculine spirituality is still in its infancy. Men are aware that images of masculinity defined by contemporary culture are inadequate. They also understand that their psychic and spiritual development has been warped by forces at work since the time of their grandfathers. So, gathered together in groups, lodges, forums, and circles, men have undertaken a quest to recover and restore authenticity, love, passion, integrity, justice and hope to the masculine soul.

2
Images of God

Is God male? Should the worship of God be limited to images that are masculine? Is the revelation of God more than the names Father, Son and Holy Spirit might indicate? Is it proper to invoke the presence of God by calling upon our "Mother, Lover and Friend"? A cursory review of most Christian theological and devotional literature would lead the reader to believe that God is male. This occurs in large part because of the way that language frames images of God.

Language is one of the building blocks of communion. It gives form to inner movements of impulse and thought, and facilitates connections necessary for personal intersections. Language names, defines, offers, symbolizes, compares and enables the ability to relate to "I" and "Thou." In other words, language provides the capacity for both self-reference and communication with others.[1] As such, any study of human relationships will necessarily include an analysis of the role that language plays in the human drama.[2] This is nowhere truer than in one's relationship with the divine. Hymnologist Brian Wren notes:

> Words matter, because for Christians, they play an important part in our relationship with God. Mystics may wordlessly contemplate God. Perhaps most Christians have mystic moments when the presence of God is so real that words would fail to praise or to

name. But more often, we pray and praise using words; and, we
dare to claim, God uses the medium of human words—in scripture
text and even in our fragile contemporary words—to speak to us.[3]

The study of masculine spirituality offers no exception to this
rule. As demonstrated in the last chapter, masculine spirituality is
an effort to connect men to a way of spirit-living that is rooted
deeply in relationships with God and creation. For men to experience a profound relationship with their God, they must be free
to "praise and name" in the power of verse and rhyme, poetry and
prose, sonnet and song. As will be demonstrated in Chapter 3,
soul images for men are evocative and require a whole range of
both emotion and God-language to support them.

Accordingly, an essential component of the study of masculine
spirituality is an examination of the way that men image God.
Since language is the way to communicate symbols and represen-
tations of the divine, an analysis of "God talk" will be fruitful. The
primary question to be answered in this chapter is, *"Is a masculine image of God necessary for masculine spirituality?"*

This chapter will examine three major themes. First, I will
examine the current method of imaging God by contemporary
theologians. This will not be an exhaustive analysis of the discussion of language, gender and God. Rather, it will be an
attempt to contextualize the dialogue as it touches the development of authentic masculine spirituality. Second, I will review
one of the most fundamental issues in masculine spirituality—
the effects of patriarchy on the development of images of God in
worship and their effect upon theology. Finally, I will consider
responses to feminist critiques regarding the use of masculine
images of God.

Naming God

God is. This is the first proposition of all monotheistic religions.
Unlike philosophical and psychological schools that suggest that
any "reality" of God exists only in the human psyche, monotheism

holds that God is primordial reality. A variety of propositions on the nature of God emanate from this first principle. Within the monotheistic traditions, God is not merely a source of energy or moral reflection, but God is being itself relating to creation. If this is so, how do people participate in the existential reality called God? Chiefly through the images provided by language.[4] Images of God provide structure to the religious imagination. They inform worship,[5] and they call for moral and ethical response.[6] The primary religious images for Christianity are embodied in the pages of the New Testament. God is addressed as a Father named "Abba," as a man named "Jesus," and as a divine Spirit named "Teacher" and "Comforter." There are a host of other images crafted by the authors of the scriptural texts, but the Trinitarian images have captured the imagination of most Christians through the ages.

There is an almost inexhaustible catalogue of contemporary theological reflection that explores the method of imaging God. Such reflection runs the spectrum. At one end are those asserting that images of God flow from a font of divine revelation, and therefore are untouchable.[7] At the other end are those who argue that any image of God is built by metaphor, and therefore is personally, culturally, and theologically relative.[8] The former considerations hold that there is something existentially constitutive and salvific in the symbols of divine revelation. As such, humankind's primary response is to relate faithfully to "true knowledge" provided by such revelation.[9] The latter considerations are attempts to be true to the essence of particular theological traditions which recognize that theology has evolved in its understanding of both God and humanity.

Quantum, historical and social sciences, including cultural anthropology, psychology, psychiatry, sociology, and mythology, have contributed voluminous material unavailable to past theological reflection on images of God. In light of these contributions, a greater appreciation of the human dimension to imaging God has emerged and theological reflection has taken a more varied and, some might add, richer course of study.[10]

An older theological tradition supported a dualistic view of the universe. It imaged a God who sits on his throne far away in heaven ruling his people on earth. This view is giving way, in some quarters, to a more monistic perspective which understands God as an integral part of the creation.[11] This turn is in large part a result of the reflections offered by the disciplines noted above, and it has the potential to radically effect the way that people image and worship God. For example, the God who is imaged as the "King of kings and Lord of lords" (1 Tim 6:15) will evoke a particular series of emotional and moral responses, whereas God who is imaged as "Mother, Lover, and Friend"[12] elicits a different way of relating to God and creation.

The debate in masculine spirituality revolves around the use of gender images of God. The following are some trends that inform this discussion. First, contemporary theological writers suggest that a particular image of God is as much an identification of ourselves as it is of the divine. Given that human knowledge is conceptual and analogical, images of God will reflect the paradigms of those doing the imaging. A Presbyterian task force on worship and images of God notes:

> It is impossible to speak about God without also making certain assumptions about human nature. The identity of the Divine is inextricably tied up in our own identity. Because of this there are serious limitations to our concepts of God, which may distort our theology. To admit this can be both threatening and liberating.[13]

The psychological dynamic of projection is a prime example of this tendency. In spiritual direction, people often bring harmful images of God to the process, and the director's task is to get them to recognize these "personal projections" so that they can move toward a more authentic experience of God.[14] It is not uncommon in working with people in direction to discover that images of God as a harsh judge, a critical taskmaster or an absent father are direct projections from experience with their parents.[15] For many, conversion to and connection with the divine is a process wherein the illusions and tyrannies of the past give way to biblical images of God as revealed in the New Testament.[16] Likewise, projection is not limited to individuals. History and archetypal psychology have demonstrated that entire faith communities and nations can identify with a particular image of God. In doing so, they direct or limit the acceptable range of worship and moral experience for the whole people.[17]

A second trend is that some theological writers such as Mary Daly, Ruth Duck and Sallie McFague suggest that a reimaging of God must occur in order to promote justice for those outside the dominant power class.[18] There is a stream of thought represented by these authors that identifies any masculine image of God with patriarchy and the oppression of women, minorities and men who don't conform to the governing cultural/religious group.[19] To these writers, there is a direct correlation between a God who is primarily imaged as masculine and injustice toward oppressed peoples.[20] Likewise, authors such as Sallie McFague, Jed Diamond and Dwight Judy have established a connection between masculine images of God and attitudes toward creation and stewardship. Those who have explored this principle maintain that as long as masculine-kingship-dominance images of God eclipse the theological landscape, then principles of stewardship and care for the resources of the earth are at risk.[21]

A third trend represented by authors such as Brian Wren and Patrick Arnold maintains that refusing to expand one's images of God runs the risk of limitation and idolatry. According to monotheistic religious traditions, idolatry is the worship of anything that is not God. In light of this, some imply that theology that accepts images of God uncritically may fall into the trap of promoting the worship of images while ignoring the God that they point to. While it is true that there is an apophatic element to the development of Hebrew and Christian theology, it is also true that, from the beginning of these traditions, human characteristics, traits and images have been used to establish the link between God and humankind.[22] The Hebrew and Christian scriptures identify God by means of a wealth of images. The bible presents a God who is so identified with creation that any number of metaphors are utilized to image the closeness and remoteness of the divine. Accordingly, to limit humankind's perception of God to masculine images inhibits the range of relationship with the holy one. Wren notes:

> No image is adequate. To select one and bow down to it is idola-
> trous. If we draw on a variety of God-images and let them balance,
> enrich and clash with one another, we shall be following the
> instincts of biblical faith and the methods of many biblical voices.
> Allowing God-images to clash is important, because it reminds us
> that we are approaching that which is beyond all images.[23]

A fourth trend suggests that significant changes in the under-standing of human nature and socio-political process have occurred and that these should influence the way that God is imaged. Some theologians such as McFague and Daly submit that using images of God that are rooted in masculine antiquity tends to speak to a cultural understanding that no longer exists. For example, since kings don't ride horses into battle anymore, to utilize such an antiquated image of God as primary tends toward irrelevance in theological reflection and personal faith. Consequently, new models or ways of imaging God are more likely to connect with people in the late twentieth century.[24]

As will be demonstrated later in this chapter, there is a "minor chord" within the symphony of the discussion articulated by Rohr, Arnold and Wren which maintains that the deconstruction of masculine images of God is not necessary. In fact, their posi-tion contends that excising male images of God from the reli-gious conscience damages the masculine psyche.

Is God a Metaphor?

Thus far, I have introduced the concept that language is the vehicle by which images and models of God are conveyed. The ways that language paints "God-pictures" is at the heart of the discussion about images of God. Metaphors are the primary way that symbols of God are crafted. Since metaphors are figures of speech founded on resemblance, it is essential to recognize that metaphorical language is not literal, but rather a figurative way of speaking. The great debate in Christian theology, and ultimately for masculine spirituality, revolves around the degree to which images of God are perceived as literal or metaphorical. A brief review of the differences between the positions of Patrick Arnold and William Oddie on the relationship between metaphor and God-language will highlight the various dichotomous views of reflecting on God.

Patrick Arnold

For Patrick Arnold, "all positive God-talk is metaphorical."[25] In a work that ultimately supports the use of masculine metaphors for God, he provides the following insights into the theological use of metaphor.

- God exists in categories beyond space and time, hence beyond language.

- Communication about God, however, must occur by using spacial and temporal language.

- "Metaphorical referents" enable the human mind to link the utterly unknowable God with familiar images.

- Metaphors, while communicating truth about God, are limited, and conceal just as much about God as they reveal.

- The human tendency is to become so attached to images of God that it is easy to forget that they are only metaphors and not expressions of literal truth.[26]

Arnold provides examples of imaging God within the biblical tradition in ways that are "not all male, not all of them even human."[27] He identifies fifty-seven different metaphors that are used by biblical writers "in bold honesty and spiritual freedom" to image this otherwise unknowable God. Certainly the use of the metaphors of "Father, Son and Holy Spirit" are the ones most common to the Christian imagination. However, Arnold encourages the development of other metaphors to strengthen one's faith. His objection to the diminution of particular masculine metaphors for God will be highlighted later in this chapter.

William Oddie

William Oddie's work *What Will Happen to God? Feminism and the Reconstruction of Christian Belief* has become a definitive reference work for conservative theologians who are engaged in the debate surrounding images of God. Oddie's thesis is that centering the discussion about images of God around metaphor is to lose the value of their existential and salvific reality.

For Oddie, God language is directional. It has both horizontal and vertical aspects. Metaphors are an example of the horizontal aspect of God language. While he recognizes the value of metaphorical theology, he sees it as having limited value for Christian thinking.

> Certainly, we can understand God in a limited way by the use of metaphor: when we say 'The Lord is my shepherd, I shall not want,' we are choosing one aspect of God's relationship with us, and illustrating it by means of a simple analogy. The use of analogical, or simply comparative language about God is useful and inevitable; but it cannot by itself take us far towards him, since the ideas thus compared are within the existing boundaries of our understanding. All we can do with this kind of language is to pile metaphor upon metaphor, but still, we will only create a more and more detailed—though possibly inaccurate—map of territory which we already occupy.[28]

The vertical feature of language about God is more of a vehicle for saying something about God than it is a way to think about being human. Oddie suggests that certain images of God in and of themselves are not metaphorical, but symbolic.[29] For example, Oddie believes that reducing the primary images of the Christian imagination, "Father, Son and Holy Spirit," to metaphor robs the tradition of existential symbols that reveal God.

> There has been in our civilization, it is not too much to say, something like a mass failure of imaginative capacity; and perhaps the most striking element in this has been a decay over recent centuries of the instinct, natural in mankind, to perceive things and actions symbolically; that is, both as they appear to us and also, and at the same time, as a part of an infinite receding tracery of associated meanings, that extends far beyond our capacity to rationalize or appreciate them.[30]

For Oddie, the development of God-language that remains metaphorical is insufficient because human reflection becomes the final arbiter of understanding.[31] Oddie suggests that the vertical level of understanding images of God is promoted by the use of language that he calls "symbols." Symbols are vertical in that they participate in the reality they point to and elicit relational response.

> A symbol acts at levels of understanding which require acceptance or rejection at deeper levels of the personality than those which can be reached by the intellect alone; and the acceptance or non-acceptance of a religious symbol is, to the extent that the symbol is central, an acceptance or rejection of the entire attitude to faith which it embodies.[32]

For Oddie, trinitarian and masculine images of God are of such a symbolic and revelatory character.[33] God has intentionally revealed himself not *like* Father, Son and Holy Spirit, but *as* Father, Son and Holy Spirit. To reduce this revelatory action of God to metaphorical analysis is to damage the essence of the Christian tradition.[34]

Both Arnold and Oddie acknowledge the critical nature of understanding the role of language in discussing images of God.

Arnold, representative of most mainstream theological reflection, recognizes that the revelatory nature of language about God is encountered through prayerful analysis and the use of metaphorical theology. Oddie, however, wants to push beyond the seeming anthropocentric control of metaphorical theology to a divinely revealed symbolism that discloses and participates in the essential nature of God.

While both positions operate from different foundational presuppositions, they provide insights that masculine spirituality can appreciate. Both schools of reflection acknowledge that 1) the use of language to image God is revelatory, and that 2) a vibrant spiritual life demands an authentic connection with life-giving images of God. As will be seen in the next chapter, much of the power of Oddie's call to return to the power of symbolic images resonates with the archetypal developments of masculine spirituality. For the purposes of understanding the dialogue surrounding gender images for God, however, Arnold would be more representative of contemporary theological opinion which places the locus of revelatory activity within the reflection of the faith community.

Given this summary of the basic suppositions of contemporary images of God, I can now begin to analyze the particular formation of images of God in masculine spirituality. Feminist theologians have demonstrated the value of feminine images of God in developing an authentic spirituality for women. These images of God have emerged from a wealth of biblical, mythological and anthropological sources. In like manner, masculine spirituality seeks to understand the value of masculine images of God. I will begin this review with the correlation between patriarchy and masculine images of God.

God Images and Patriarchy

In the lexicon of gender studies, there is no word more loaded with emotional content than patriarchy. As noted above, theologians such as Mary Daly, Rosemary Radford Ruether, and Sallie

McFague criticize patriarchy, while theologians such as William Oddie and Patrick Arnold defend this socio-political paradigm and its effects upon the human saga. Patriarchy, or "The Rule of the Fathers," has been the dominant social structure in the west from at least the second millennium B.C.E. to the present.[35] Arnold notes that "in social roles such as father, tribal elder, judge, priest, and king, males have guided society for millennia, creating law and order, empires and institutions."[36] The Hebrew tradition is replete with examples of the patriarch exercising wise (and sometimes not so wise) leadership over the tribe or nation. Abraham, Isaac and Jacob are the preeminent examples of the archetypal patriarch. As illustrated in the Hebrew scriptures, the patriarch's role was to lead not only his immediate family, but also his clan in political, sociological, economic and religious activity. While the role of the patriarch diminished in the ancient Near East, there is no dispute that male-dominated leadership has been the norm throughout subsequent human history.

Patriarchy, with few exceptions, is the normative paradigm of socio-political operation in the west to this day. For the purposes of these reflections, the definition of patriarchy is simple: *Patriarchy is a masculine dominance of the interpretation of reality.* An exegetical demonstration of patriarchal assumptions will be helpful to understand its influence on the development of masculine images of God. First, patriarchal ways of thinking and knowing are the only accepted mediators of reality. Second, the adversarial nature of patriarchy views those outside the dominant class (usually women and minorities) as threatening the social structure, therefore inferior and dangerous. Third, to enforce the patriarchal paradigm, control is exercised by the dominant class over forces perceived as oppositional. Fourth, the acceptable assumptions of patriarchy are ensured by the exercise of power.[37]

With the advent of gender studies in theology, patriarchal ways of thinking have come under scrutiny. The "manifestation and institutionalization of male dominance over women and children in the family, and the extension of male dominance over women in society in general"[38] reflect the collective standard by which critics judge patriarchy. Gillette and Moore see patriarchy as "an attack on masculinity in its fullness as well as femininity in its fullness."[39] It should be noted that in archetypal psychology, there is a great appreciation for the archetypes of the "patriarch" and "matriarch," and that these should not be confused with the socio-political nature of patriarchy outlined above. I will examine the role of archetypes in some depth in Chapter 3.

Due to the richness of theological reflection, there are those who are willing to recognize that patriarchy has a "shadow side," but suggest that there is a long history of beneficence to humanity due, in large part, to patriarchal leadership. Arnold submits:

> Its modern critics rightly point to its historic and present abuses such as rigidity, domination, misogyny, and violence. Yet the storm of abuse raining on patriarchy is also in many ways uncritical; it is unfair, unscholarly, and unwise only to characterize a system by its abuses. One rarely hears a genuinely critical account of patriarchy that also takes into account its vast contributions to human history; the word is used invariably in a highly polemical and political fashion.[40]

In spite of the diversity of views on the consequences of patriarchy, there is agreement that it has affected men's thinking, relationships and prayers. Men think, act, relate, work, and pray in ways that have been formed in a patriarchal culture, so to understand the development of imaging God for men, one must understand something of the masculine approach to life.

Masculinity and Patriarchy

The following are generally accepted characteristics that are predominant in, but not limited to, men. Theories surrounding the etiology of such personality characteristics are the subject of debates chronicled elsewhere.[41] For the purposes of this study, whether by "nature or nurture," the following are traits commonly identified as masculine.

• Competitiveness
• Independence and Autonomy
• Responsibility and Accountability
• Linear Thinking
• Provincial Orientation
• Action Orientation
• Production Orientation
• Body-Soul Dualism
• Phallocentric Orientation
• Control and Order

The above inventory implies that a man's approach to life is very oriented toward "doing, direction and definition."[42] A man's focus is outward, he takes great satisfaction in accomplishment, and tends toward the concrete and experiential in ways of knowing.[43] As such, common masculine paradigms have a certain "distance and hardness" to their orientation. Societies and theologies that are "man-driven" can be expected to mirror both the strengths and weaknesses of these personality traits in the composition of norms and premises.

Patriarchal society values these traits of masculinity and establishes them as the "norms" for access to power, prestige and position. Ruth Duck notes:

> The very structure of language in patriarchal cultures reflects the patriarchal pyramid of power, making invisible or devaluing women, people of color, people of differing abilities, and any who are not dominant in society.[44]

The defect of this form of socio-political process, and its influence on the development of theology, is that it represents only half the mystery of humanity. Patriarchy is fearful of anything non-masculine, and as such denigrates the necessary feminine presence, both in the world and within itself.[45] It is from this perspective of male dominance that feminist calls for justice and gender equality emanate.

Those involved in the study of masculine spirituality grapple with issues of wholeness and relationship. As noted previously, for a man to be on the "God-path" he must learn to relate to God, himself, his neighbor and creation in ways that are unitive, but uniquely masculine. Patriarchy, with its stereotypical way of defining masculinity, doesn't provide men an opportunity to experience unitive wholeness, as it is too enmeshed into the "shadow side" of the masculine psyche to encourage growth and emancipation. Moore and Gillette note:

> In our view, patriarchy is not the expression of deep and rooted masculinity, for truly deep and rooted masculinity is not abusive. Patriarchy is the expression of the immature masculine. It is the expression of Boy psychology, and, in part, the shadow—or crazy—side of masculinity. It expresses the stunted masculine, fixated at immature levels.[46]

As noted earlier in this chapter, psychological projection is a human tendency to attribute particular qualities or traits onto another. Patriarchy is an example of a collective psychological projection onto God of a set of personality attributes. The patriarchal view of God looks suspiciously similar to the socio-political realities of ancient monarchies. Judgment, rule, control, punishment, sovereignty and dominance are the hallmarks of images of God that are enslaved to patriarchy.

By conducting a critical review of the essential sociological and theological characteristics of the patriarchal paradigm, Brian Wren has developed a "Portrait of a Patriarchal God."[47] In it, he depicts an image of God that would emerge from the religious imagination of a patriarchal society. To summarize the work:

- The patriarchal God is in control of everything. He may or may not allow a great deal of freedom for his subjects, but ultimately, he controls all creation.

- The patriarchal God sits on top of a relationship pyramid. Imaged as king, or dictator, he is the ultimate "monarch"...one who rules alone. He rules by command and decree, expects submission and obedience, and offers punishment or mercy in response to transgression.

• The patriarchal God is almighty and omnipotent. He is strong, active and triumphant. He conquers all that stands in his way. Since omnipotence enables this God to claim all as his creation, he is transcendent, distant from creation. Creation becomes a commodity, and not a locus of relationship.

• The patriarchal God is in control. He is invulnerable, impassive and impassable.

• The patriarchal God is male and masculine. Any feminine qualities of the patriarchal God would be seen as inferior and ancillary to his essence.

Theological Assumptions of Patriarchy

The effects of patriarchy upon the development of authentic masculine spirituality are profound. As illustrated above, patriarchal images of God lead to suppositions which impact men and their relationship to the divine and to their community. Karen Bloomquist comments upon some of the basic assumptions of patriarchal paradigms for theology.

Dualism. Patriarchy operates out of a very dualistic framework. It experiences the transcendent as dichotomized from the immanent; spirit is separate from matter; creation is separate from creator; and a "masculine" God is separate from "feminized" believers. Patriarchal consciousness is very either/or and has difficulty with both/and modes of experience.

Hierarchy. In order to communicate with a transcendent God, one must develop a hierarchy of relationships. God is in "his" heaven, and "his" subjects are on earth, fulfilling "his" will. This works in reverse as well—the patriarchal paradigm operates out of a hierarchical system of relationships toward others. Consequently, it is necessary that people "know their place" within the social structure. This enables ordering and control by the dominant class.

Power. In patriarchy, power is God's ability to accomplish his will. The power to accomplish, therefore, is power to control. If the patriarchal way of ordering relationships is within the context of hierarchy, then the exercise of power is necessary to effect such ordering.[48]

Aloneness. God, dualistically separate from the world, is characterized as "apart" and hence "transcendent." Aloneness, impassibility and autonomy characterize much of the common masculine experience today, and a patriarchal paradigm of God reinforces this stereotypical activity.

For a spirituality to serve as an authentic vehicle for masculine development, it must connect men to God and to others. A patriarchal view of God sees only a permanent dualism between God and creation, thereby encouraging a similar separation of men from the rest of nature. Consequently, the messages communicated by patriarchal theology are harmful to men, women and creation. In light of this, the work of gender studies in theology takes on a greater urgency as the need for a more holistic view of God and humankind becomes evident.

This review has highlighted some of the limitations of the effect of patriarchy upon the development of images of God for men. Patriarchal paradigms as typified above lead men away from relationship and back into patterns that value isolation over community, autonomy over cooperation, masculine personality characteristics over feminine, and control over growth. The challenge, therefore, for masculine spirituality is to 1) recognize those places where destructive elements of patriarchy have taken hold in attitudes toward God and others, 2) engage in the struggle for justice in the area of gender relationships, and 3) immerse itself in the study of masculine images of God that will lead men toward the depths of their being.

A Man's God

Having demonstrated contemporary assumptions about the process and development of images of God and the effects of patriarchal paradigms upon them, we now ask, *How can a man who is committed to wholeness and justice worship a masculine God?* Implicit in this question is the need to explore the relationship between masculine and feminine images of God, and the question of inclusion and exclusion of either in a man's worship experience.

Discussions about masculine images of God by men must be contexualized within the framework of justice and freedom. Recall that contemporary theology has opened the door for women to experience the liberating presence of feminine images of God. But post-feminist studies which seek to provide the same degree of freedom for men are met in the theological community with critical ambivalence at best or outright hostility at worst. Part of this is rooted in the fear that a return by men to masculine images of God means a return to patriarchal assumptions and domination of women. But the consensus of the contemporary theological community is that patriarchy, the socio-political paradigm of men's dominance over women, is destructive to the image of God for both genders.

Appropriately, the challenge for the development of masculine spirituality is twofold. It must first celebrate the theological development and freedom of feminist theology. Rejoicing with women in the fruitfulness of their theological endeavor, men can learn from their struggle and support their effort to develop feminine images of God. Second, it must then press on to cultivate new understandings of the treasury of masculine images of God found in the tradition. To do any less would subordinate the essential goodness of authentic masculinity and succumb to a reverse-patriarchy, that which accepts only the feminist exegesis of reality. Culbertson echoes this challenge when he writes:

> The women's movement is light-years ahead of the men's movement, and much that has been achieved by feminism has hap-

pened because women went away from men to work through
their issues. The time has now come for men to go away from
women to do our homework within the intentional community of
sensitive men. Until we have sorted through a number of critical
same-sex identity issues, we are not ready to build a new future
of men and women together. We must build on sameness before
we are ready to build on differences.[49]

This "new future" must include reflections about images of
God that speak to the Christian imagination of both men and
women. Theological paradigms which encourage men and
women to have "their" respective gods without developing uni-
fying images for the entire tradition will produce insipid and
provincial spirituality, a hallmark of the patriarchal mind-set.
Given the priority of the assembly in Christian worship, liturgical theology is challenged to image God in ways that include and
enliven, rather than exclude and dampen.

Masculine spirituality examines the use of masculine images
of God from a participatory perspective. It is a spirituality that is
personal, evocative, challenging and compelling. Since men's
approach to life is rooted in "doing, direction and definition,"
theological reflection upon experience becomes an important
element of a man's spirituality. It is not a spirituality that is anti-
feminine, but it celebrates the revelation of God through men and
masculinity. As the study of masculine spirituality is developing,
there is much evidence available to demonstrate that men have
deep capacities for relationship, community, loyalty and commitment. Consequently, images of God that communicate deeply to
men will pursue the connection between the masculine and the
divine in two dimensions: connection and challenge.

Connection

Trinitarian images of "Father, Son and Holy Spirit" are the
most familiar to men. As such, while the majority of men don't
find them offensive, neither do they invoke a worshipful
response. Arnold notes:

Modern religion is severely restricted in its available God-metaphors. No wonder our sermons, worship services, and spiritual books are often so boring; we have confined ourselves to pitifully few metaphors—Lover and Father, primarily.[50]

Those who work with men note the disconnection between contemporary men and spirituality. Part of this disconnection is because men are not "taught" to have a spiritual life; therefore, spirituality is reduced to religious practice. This convention ensures that men lose interest once their notions of obligation are satisfied. Some authors suggest that the "traditional" images of God are so overworn that they have lost any power to reveal and connect. Masculine spirituality seeks to develop creative ways of connecting men to symbols of God so that insights into conversion might occur. Rituals, drumming circles, men's gatherings and a renewed interest in telling the stories of ancient images of God are ways that facilitate reconnections. Teaching men how to relate to God as Father, Wildman, King, Son, Warrior, Judge, Lord, and Brother so as to experience their evocative power is a formative challenge to the development of spirituality.

The importance of masculine images is that they reveal a God to whom men can relate. As legitimate as it may be theologically to call God "Mother," men by and large have little relationship with mother-energy. But a man can readily identify with the challenging images of men and masculine activity. The richness of masculine metaphors in the scriptures is striking. An evaluation of these images suggests that they can be used by men to deepen their relationship with God.[51] Since it has been established that images are the vehicle for the revelation of the divine, masculine images can make God known in ways that are conceptually and instinctually familiar to men. In other words, masculine images of God can bridge the theological chasm and make the transcendent God knowable and immanent to men.[52]

Challenge

In addition to providing men with divine connections, masculine images of God issue a challenge to the assumptions of postmodern men. Since patriarchal ways of knowing have limited the ability of men to develop authentic spirit, masculine spirituality attempts to challenge and to be challenged by the male metaphors of God within the tradition. Culbertson notes:

> In short, the traditional literatures of theology and spirituality are so dominated by culturally conditioned male assumptions that they provide too narrow a range of options for men to explore either the fullness of human spiritual capacity or the richness of the godhead.[53]

Some of the masculine images for God in the scriptures are considered offensive to contemporary sensibilities, i.e., God as a destroyer, a thief, an executioner, a jealous lover, a seducer, etc.[54] Yet, contemplation on such images can prove worthwhile. When a man grapples with the challenge of these images, profound transformation can occur. Interaction with offensive images can lead men to the path of integration as they 1) attend to the conflicts that these images raise within them, and 2) examine the assumptions that have fueled their response to the images. Men's groups report that as they contend with some of these images in group meditation, members of the group have experienced moments of profound insight. Wren writes:

> It therefore seems true to biblical faith to use strong and vivid God images in considerable variety. Then we can let each image have full impact on our imagination before moving on to another which may connect or clash with it.[55]

His call to "connecting and clashing" symbols challenges men to examine their assumptions regarding relationships with God and others. An honest encounter with disturbing masculine images can reform a way that a man thinks about God. Richard Rohr notes:

> Christians forget that God in the Old Testament comes off much wilder than he does in the New Testament. Right at the beginning of the Bible in the Book of Genesis, he looks down from heaven and doesn't like the way people are living, so decides to flood them out and start over again. That's wild![56]

God the "wildman" challenges the for-profit corporate masculinity of western civilization, God the "Magician" thrusts scientific rationalism into dispute, and God the "Lover" contests the masculine obsession of sexual conquest and homoerotic fear that destroys masculine intimacy. So whether offensive to the contemporary mind or not, masculine images provide a challenge that men understand: the challenge of conquest, of struggle and ultimately of union.

In contra-distinction to some feminist theologians, no writer in the arena of masculine spirituality suggests that excising masculine images of the divine from a man's religious imagination is a wise undertaking.[57] The degree to which masculine images are given priority in religious reflections will vary, but all the authors surveyed suggest that masculine spirituality must struggle to elicit a new appreciation of the revelation of God in man. Masculinity is a reflection of God, and as such it is good. The abundance of masculine images offers glimpses into the robust possibilities available to men as they seek to envision a new way of relating, which is the ultimate goal of spirituality.

Summary

The question which gave direction to this chapter was: *"Is a masculine God necessary for masculine spirituality?"* The answer is "yes." To show how this is so, I have reviewed images of God offered by contemporary theologians. Metaphorical theology has enabled those painting "God pictures" to understand better the relationship between language, images of God, and evolving concepts of revelation. The positions of Patrick Arnold and William Oddie demonstrated the diversity of theological reflection in this regard.

I then turned to an overview of the impact of patriarchy upon the formation of images of God. A review of the literature demonstrated that masculine ways of thinking, knowing and acting aren't necessarily patriarchal. To illustrate the impact of patriarchy upon images of God and theology, I offered a review of the critical analysis of Brian Wren and Karen Bloomquist in this regard. Both authors illustrated how male dominant images of God vitiate the varied and holistic images of God available for worship and reflection.

Finally I conducted a review of the ways that masculine images of God can be used in men's spirituality. While recognizing the need for freedom in the imaging process, the study of masculine symbols of God demonstrated that there is connection and challenge available to men who interact with them.

The conclusion of the authors represented in these pages is that masculine images of God are a rich source of reflection for men. To eradicate them from the religious consciousness would be as great an act of gender-violence as any ever perpetrated by patriarchy.

3
Soul Images of a Man

Masculine spirituality has been characterized as a "questing" process. At its heart, it is an invitation to participate in experiences of masculine identification and exploration. Men's studies have demonstrated that contemporary men, long disconnected from the rhythms of nature and relationships, need an inward journey. Masculine spirituality is a way for men to identify and connect with their deepest energies through ritual and discussion, feeling and action. The process of helping men discover and become familiar with their depths has been named "soul work." Men committed to "the quest" must participate in this sometimes frightening journey into their own depths:

- to recognize archetypal energy.
- to befriend the "shadow" or repressed parts of their personality.
- to grieve lost opportunities and love.

Sam Keen writes:

The Soulful Quest...is a pilgrimage into the depths of the self. We leave the sunlit world of easy roles and prefabricated tokens of masculinity, penetrate the character armor, get beneath the personality, and plunge into the chaos and pain of the old "masculine" self. This isn't the fun part of the trip. It's spelunking in

Plato's cave, feeling our way through the illusions we have mistaken for reality, crawling through the drain sewers where the for-
bidden "unmanly" feelings dwell, confronting the demons and
dark shadows that have held us captive from their underground
haunts.[1]

These "underground haunts" are a metaphorical description of
the dwelling place of a man's energies, his soul. This illustrates
the influence of depth psychology on the development of masculine spirituality. Clinical and philosophical insights into the
human personality have influenced the growth of this spirituality in a profound way. Most of the authors writing about men have
adopted Jungian paradigms to define the development of the
masculine soul. As such, when masculine spirituality affirms the
significance of "soul work," it adopts fundamental Jungian
assumptions about men and their psychic construct.[2]

In this chapter I will address the fundamental issues of the
exploration of men's souls. First I review contemporary understandings of the soul. Then I examine the basic premises of
archetypal psychology and analyze the way that mythic language
and story are used in masculine spirituality. Next I consider the
way that the "familiar myths and roadmaps of masculinity"[3] are
used in the men's movement in order to review the preeminent
archetypes of masculine spirituality. Then I will summarize three
myths of masculine soulful identity and development, "The
Quest for the Holy Grail," "Iron John," and "White Snake."
These myths contribute to an understanding of the mythic and
archetypal ways that men move toward experiencing their lost
heritage of passion and depth.

The Meaning of Soul

If a fundamental objective of masculine spirituality is to invite
men to soulful living, we need to understand the "soul" which
men are to discover. John Bradshaw summarizes popular concepts of "the soul" when he says:

People often search their soul to find their innocence or their dream. Those going through arduous trials are often told that their soul is on trial. Those who act in a cruel and merciless way are called soulless. We have soul music and soul food. Those who seem hopelessly addicted, those who are chronic criminals, are called lost souls. We hear talk of troubled souls, old souls, innocent souls, and inspired souls. Many religions believe in the immortality of the soul. Some also believe that one's soul can be possessed by the devil or possessed by evil spirits.[4]

In other words, there are a myriad of popular and philosophical understandings of the soul. Helpful perspectives of the soul have emerged from the inter-disciplinary strides in the study of mythology, psychology, theology and sociology. Thomas Moore, a Jungian therapist and "expert" on the soul, summarizes this outlook when he writes: "Soul is not a thing, but a quality or a dimension of experiencing life and ourselves. It has to do with depth, value, relatedness, heart and personal substance."[5]

There is a resurgence of interest surrounding the soul in contemporary philosophical, psychological and spiritual writing. In a post-modern, high-tech society bereft of soul, many seek to reclaim the art of soulful living. The reflections of theorists like Carl Jung, James Hillman, Robert Sardello, John Bradshaw, Sam Keen and Thomas Moore have contributed much to contemporary understanding of the soul. Moore writes:

> It is impossible to define precisely what the soul is. Definition is an intellectual enterprise anyway, the soul prefers to imagine. We know intuitively that soul has to do with genuineness and depth, as when we say that certain music has soul or a remarkable person is soulful.[6]

Bradshaw states simply, "Soulfulness is not fully definable because it is a state of being. It is the state of being fully human."[7] Moore supports this insight naming the soul, "a quality or dimension of experiencing life and ourselves."[8]

In *Re-Visioning Psychology*, James Hillman discerns three dimensions to soul:

> First, soul refers to the deepening of events into experience; second, the significance soul makes possible, whether in love or in religious concern, derives from its special relation with death. And third, by soul I mean the imaginative possibility in our natures, the experiencing through reflective speculation, dream, image, and fantasy—that mode which recognizes all realities...as primarily symbolic or metaphorical.[9]

Evidence of the soul can be found in a person's dreams, values, relationships, music, body and feelings. It is discovered in their preferences, work, pathos, environment, disease, spirituality, and eros. It breaks forth in "every aspect of life."[10] Contrary to some of the popular notions described above, soul is more than the experience of feeling, it is an experience of imagination, perception, emotion, inspiration, and intuition.

In an attempt to clarify some of the semantic confusion surrounding the soul, authors distinguish between traditional categories of soul and spirit. Daniel Noel observes:

> Soul, from this point of view, is distinct from spirit, which is seen as overlapping with mind, as the German word *geist* suggests. Spirit favors detached abstractness, purity, and unity, all characteristics that transcend earth and body and their sensuous imagery. Soul, on the other hand, thrives on attachments and imaginings, the concrete and sensual, immanent meaning, multiplicity, and imperfection that characterize earth and body.[11]

This resonates with a renewed biblical anthropology of the three dimensions of the human person. Richard Rohr summarizes a historical review of the biblical perspectives of the soul:

• In the Hebrew Scriptures, the human person was envisioned as body, soul and spirit.

- In the Christian Scriptures there was a tendency to blend the soul and the spirit into one existential reality. Accordingly, soul and spirit became interchangeable terms.

- As dualism took root in the developing church, the "spirit" which was eternal was considered good, and the "flesh," which was corruptible, was bad. This is based in part upon St. Paul's attempt to contextualize the hold that the immediate (the flesh) held on a person. This blocked one's ability to be open to the "spirit" which was transcendent and universal.

- As a result of this theological distinction, the "soul" became that eternal part of a person that is either "saved" and goes to heaven, or "lost" and goes to hell. All "spiritual" activity of the church revolves around "saving" the souls of its members.[12]

This dualistic notion of body versus spirit continues in some circles today, but biblical scholarship has demonstrated that a more "biblical" understanding of the human person is a unified relationship of body, soul and spirit. The human being is not an embodied spirit, but rather a unified relationship of three dimensions of existence.

A summary of this anthropology suggests that a person's spirit is that dimension of human existence which is open to transcendent and universal experiences of God. It provides the capacity for experience and union beyond the individual psyche. In other words, "Spirit in you seeks Spirit in God."[13] The soul provides the capacity to lead inward, toward a person's fundamental psychic structure: into meaning and symbolism, emotions and dream. The energy of the soul animates a person and gives him or her the capacity for authentic living.[14] Since the goal of spirituality is the development of authentic, grounded relationships, Bradshaw reflects on how being grounded in soul enables one to be open to spirit.

Soulfulness leads to spirituality. Spirituality is a state of fullness, an amplitude. With spirituality we see with a larger vision. The whole comes into view....Soulfulness leads us to the realization that spirituality is our human destiny. To be fully human is to be fully spiritual. Soul sees the depth of spirituality in everything and everyone.[15]

Moore notes that counselors are discovering that the soul is not subject to therapeutic jurisdiction.

Soul is the font of who we are, and yet it is far beyond our capacity to devise and to control. We can cultivate, tend, enjoy, and participate in the things of the soul, but we can't outwit it or manage it or shape it to the designs of a willful ego.[16]

He suggests that part of the soul's sovereignty is rooted in its role as mediator between the multiple realms of human existence. "Tradition teaches that soul lies midway between understanding and unconsciousness, and that its instrument is neither the mind, nor the body, but the imagination."[17] Rohr proposes that this elusiveness is illustrated in the word *psyche* itself. He notes that "originally the word for psyche meant butterfly. That's how ephemeral and hard it is to get a hold of soul, but it is precisely the soul that makes the unconscious, conscious."[18]

Finally, the body is the place where soul is fused with spirit, and the person is present to the world.[19] The body holds a somatic wisdom that has been disdained in western culture, and soul work invites men into a relationship with their body, its history and knowledge.[20] The value of increasing bodily awareness for men will be specifically examined in the next chapter.

This holistic model of the human being places great value in the development of the entire person. As such, great care and attention is paid to the way that the soul expresses itself. In psychotherapy this entails a shift in practice from "cure" to "care,"[21] and in medicine, this suggests developing a greater understanding of the connection between symptoms and the soulful information they are trying to provide.[22] In spirituality, attention to soul results in a greater appreciation of a wider field of experience by which one relates to God. Dreams, passions, longings, emotions, obsessions, and attachments become a vehicle for the revelation of God's incarnation in the human person. Ritual is an important part of this soulful attention to spirituality. Its value for men will be discussed in Chapter 5.

Any developing masculine spirituality must lead men into "soul work." The tenants of archetypal psychology suggest that there are numerous facets to a man's soul. The *logos*, or masculine dimension of his soul, is familiar ground. There he experiences familiar movements of mind and action. The *anima* or feminine dimension of his soul consists of images, feelings, stories, poetry, passions, attachments, etc.

Soul work plunges men into the unfamiliar psychic and spiritual territory of their undeveloped essence. Its promise of a new quality of life lures men into "deep caverns" of primal energy which seek release. It moves men beyond ego-control into the domain of the unconscious where men confront repressed psychic material. This, in turn, opens the door to greater levels of awareness and relationship.[23]

"Soul work" holds great value for masculine spirituality. As men discover soul, they are more likely candidates for a full participation in the reconstruction of society. As noted in the last chapter, patriarchy is a manifestation of "Boy Psychology," the stunted masculine.[24] In this socio-political paradigm, men are locked into "outer" (masculine) modes of knowledge and action, shying away from anything considered feminine (inner). Feminist critiques of men are often centered around their inability to connect with their "feeling side." According to this appraisal, thousands of years of masculinity gone awry is evidence of the disconnection of men from their feelings.

Soul work thrusts men into the arena of feeling and intuition, of interaction with particular emotions and undeveloped psychic energy. Through soul work men are discovering a richness in themselves beyond description. Men's psychic and physical well-being also demand this soul work. Until men are allowed to experience the torrents of soul stirring within, they will be subject to the passing whims of the shadow that is repressed psychic energy.[25] This in turn can result in crippling physical and mental illness. Soul work integrates the various parts of a man's personality, and this leads to more robust physical and mental health.

Archetype and Myth

As noted previously in this chapter, masculine spirituality has adopted Jungian paradigms of development to explain the psychological evolution of men.[26] No other model of human development explains the unfolding of masculine spirituality in such a profound way. It recognizes all human experience as authentic to the psyche. Accordingly, there is great interest in the way that archetypal psychology and mythology are utilized to explain men's thoughts, feelings and actions.

Carl Jung, the founder of depth psychology, placed great value upon the "mysteries of the human soul."[27] Drawing upon the work of Sigmund Freud, Jung expanded the arena of psychological reflection to include the exploration of the relationship between the person and transpersonal consciousness. His work is being accepted more widely in the practice of contemporary Christian spirituality. The prayerful adaptation of practices such as dreamwork, guided imagery, befriending the shadow, and embracing the anima/animus all owe their genesis to Jung's contemplation.

Nowhere is Jung's influence more profoundly recognized than in the area of archetypal psychology and its subsequent impact upon spiritual practice. The relationship between archetypal psychology and the men's movement is being chronicled by authors such as Robert Bly, Robert Moore and Douglas Gillette, Jed Diamond, Dwight Judy, Patrick Arnold, Richard Rohr, Jean Shinoda Bolen, and Aaron Kipnis. By way of introduction, Arnold notes:

Jung showed that we cannot understand or successfully come to terms with our own spiritual issues without relating them to the language of our own unconscious and the inherited collective unconscious of humanity as expressed in the powerful myths that pervade human storytelling.[28]

The Power of Archetypes

Jung's clinical practice convinced him that each person experiences a relationship between the inner and outer worlds through interaction with universal images, or archetypes. Arnold observes:

In one of his most fruitful insights, Jung realized that his patients' dreams often contained symbols and figures signifying much more than the particular individual issues each faced. Jung recognized in these dreams striking similarities to the classic themes, patterns, and motifs of the world's greatest art, its oldest myths and stories, and even its most profound religions.[29]

These reflections led to Jung's theory of archetypes. Bolen offers a helpful definition: *"Archetypes are preexistent, or latent, internally determined patterns of being and behaving, or perceiving and responding. These patterns are contained in a collective unconscious—that part of the unconscious that is not individual, but universal or shared."*[30] In other words, archetypes are the "hard-wired components of our genetically transmitted psychic machine,"[31] which are charged with psychic energy (libido), and symbolize life experiences common to all humankind.

Jung suggested that archetypes arise from the "collective unconscious." He proposed that the collective unconscious is a common human memory transmitted genetically to each generation; and it is from this memory that primary and instinctive patterns of archetypes emerge.[32] Moore and Gillette note that in developing his theory of the collective unconscious, Jung placed the locus of archetypal structures within this transpersonal "memory" of the entire human race.[33] This was based on his study of the universality of dreams, symbols, images and myths which transcend culture and era. As Arnold suggests, these images occur in every culture and time:

> These patterns, or archetypes are "richly varied motifs" that may appear in the dreams of an African child or the ghost stories of a Japanese raconteur, in the sand-paintings of a Navajo shaman or the rituals of a Roman liturgy, in the mythology of the Hindu religion or in the awesome primitive etchings of a Paleolithic cave.[34]

Archetypes and Mythic Image

One of the basic premises of Jung's psychology was that archetypes must be universal images since they reflect common human tendencies which have been enshrined throughout history in mythic form. Bolen notes: "Because archetypal images are part of our collective inheritance, they are familiar."[35] They are so familiar, in fact, that they are typified in the personalized images of mythology. There are a variety of mythic forms for Jungian studies in general, and masculine studies in particular. The following demonstrates the variety of mythological forms used to illustrate the influence of archetypes upon men:

- Jean Bolen in her book, *Gods in Everyman*, reflects upon the way that a study of the Olympian gods reveal archetypes in men. She suggests that men can access Zeus energy, or be possessed by Dionysian ecstasy. To Bolen, each man carries a predominant "god-image" from Olympus within him. The path to masculine maturity lies in accessing and transcending the archetypal energies.

- In *Knights Without Armor*, Kipnis portrays the power of the archetypes for men in his representation of the sky and earth gods of pre-Christian history. He outlines the ways that ancient societies honored a plethora of divinity that included earth gods as well as sky gods, fecund lovers as well as warriors. Kipnis suggests that each man come to identify the movements of the variety of deities within.[36]

• Patrick Arnold provides a survey of archetypes using images of biblical mythology in *Wildmen, Warriors and Kings*. Arnold illustrates various archetypal energy patterns present in men through the stories of Abraham, Moses, Solomon, Elijah, Elisha, Jeremiah, Jonah and Jesus.[37]

Robert Moore and Douglas Gillette offer an example of specifically Jungian explorations into the structure of a man's psyche. In their series of books, grounded in both theology and mythology, the authors demonstrate the beneficence of Jung's insights for masculine psychology and spirituality. To Moore/Gillette, archetypes are the foundational imprints upon a man's psyche:

> It is our experience that deep within every man are blueprints, what we can also call "hard wiring" for the calm and positive mature masculine. Jungians refer to these masculine potentials as archetypes, or primordial images.[38]

These dynamic energies are part of the structural foundation of the masculine psyche. They are rooted at the level of animal instinct and transcend both local culture and tradition.

By way of a brief introduction into a Jungian understanding of a man's psyche, Moore/Gillette suggest:

• At the foundational level of each man's psyche there is a "transcendent Self."

• The "Self" is a man's psychic center. As such, it is the reconciling point for all psychologically dynamic opposites.[39] The "Self" is the truest essence of a man's being.

• While Jungian psychology holds that the Self is androgynous, Moore and Gillette suggest that for most men, the Self manifests itself as masculine.

• While it is the deepest essence of a man's personality, there are other facets to his psychic structure which interact with the Self. The Ego is that part of the psyche which provides a sense of personal identification. As the authors note, "When people talk about the Ego, they usually mean the 'I' we normally think of as ourselves. The Ego is who we believe ourselves to be, the part of our psyche we identify with our name."[40]

Archetypal energy is distinct from, but interacts with, the Ego within a man's psychic structure. Moore and Gillette note that the encounter with "transpersonal masculine" images occurs at the Ego-archetype axis. When an archetype arises within a man, its locus of mediation is Ego-consciousness. "A man's blending of human and 'divine' energies is essentially the experience of what we are calling an Ego-archetype axis."[41] The manner in which the archetype emerges depends in large part upon the degree of Ego maturity and its ability to transcend the shadow aspects of the archetype.[42]

Archetypes are "bedrock structures" that define the psyche's own nature and, as such, represent transpersonal human psychological characteristics. A man's relation to archetypes is not merely one of curious intellectual engagement. It is an encounter with independent and powerful energies that influence and captivate one's soul. To illustrate this, Moore/Gillette note:

For any individual the archetypes may be creative and life-enhancing or destructive and death-dealing. The result depends in part on how the Ego is able to relate to them based on its own developmental history. Properly accessing and using the Libido available to the psyche amount to a sort of psychological technology. If we learn the technology and use it properly, we can use the energy to make generative men and women of ourselves. But if we fail to learn how to use these vast energy resources, or misuse them, we will be courting our own destruction, and we may take others with us.[43]

Moore/Gillette have identified four major forms of masculine energy common to the universal experience of men. Allowing history and myth to illustrate the presence of these four archetypes, they demonstrate the need to identify with, access and transcend these images. The potential for each man is a calm centeredness, committed determination, profound transformation and deep joy. These potentialities are made possible by the energy provided by the archetypes of King, Warrior, Magician and Lover.

Each of these archetypal energies constitute a major part of a man's psyche. Gillette/Moore point to the "fourfold quadrant" of the masculine psyche typified in myth and literature.[44] As such, the archetypes overlap and enrich each other: "A good King is always also a Warrior, a Magician, and a Lover."[45] The following is a brief review of these four archetypes and their effects upon men.

The King

The King is the primary archetype of the masculine psyche.[46] Moore and Gillette note that at its highest, the King archetype comes close to being "god in his masculine form within every man."[47] The other three major masculine archetypes, the Warrior, the Magician and the Lover, all flow from the King.[48] The King is the archetypal energy of centeredness and security within a man. For men, therefore, accessing the King archetype is to move away from disorder and chaos and into stability and calm, away from impotence and sterility and into creative and fecund masculine energy.

The King archetype in its fullness possesses the qualities of order, of reasonable and rational planning, of integration and integrity in the masculine psyche. It stabilizes chaotic emotion and out-of-control behaviors. It gives stability and centeredness, it mediates vitality, life-force and joy.[49]

Due to the difference in socio-political paradigms of the late twentieth century, there is a dearth of king images in contemporary society. Fathers are the most familiar image that most men have for "big men," that is, men who exude king-like energy. The authors demonstrate, however, that, while underlying the Father archetype, the King is more basic and expansive than the Father, hence eclipsing it.

The King archetype establishes boundaries for the psyche. History, literature and myth demonstrate that one of the functions of both human kings and "King-Gods" was to bring order from chaos and establish the "right order of things."[50] Moore/Gillette point to a compelling illustration of this in the clinical practice of John W. Perry.

> Perry…discovered the King's power to heal by reorganizing the personality in the dreams and visions of schizophrenic patients. In psychotic episodes, and in other liminal states of mind, images of the sacred King would rush up from the depths of his patients' unconscious.…These King images were immensely organizing, ordering and creatively healing.[51]

In addition to ordering psychic reality, the King is the source of fertility and blessing for a man's personality. The King produces libido or life energy for a man. When a man accesses the King, he experiences vitality, life-force, joy, balance and blessing.[52] Just as a good earthly king blesses his subjects, so too does the archetypal King produce a sense of blessing and positive self-valuation for a man. The King leads a man to peace and stability, growth and leadership for himself first, and then for others.

Each of these four archetypes has a bi-polar shadow to its expression. When a man doesn't properly access the archetype in its fullness, he will experience one of its bi-polar manifestations.

In the case of the King archetype, the bi-polar shadow has been named the Shadow King: Tyrant or Weakling. The active pole of the Shadow is a manifestation of energy within a man which releases a tyrannical spirit within. By way of example, the Tyrant is typified in King Herod of biblical mythology. In the gospel narrative, the Shadow King engineers a mass execution of children to stop the ascendence of the Christ child. This spirit has reigned throughout much of history, as the last two world wars and the tyranny of countless dictators of both the right and left illustrate. Possessed by their own grandiosity, men hate, fear and envy anything that threatens their realms, and they move to control or destroy it.

The passive pole of the Shadow King is the Weakling. When a man is in the grip of the Weakling, he abdicates any kingly role and willingly submits to whatever prevalent psychic energy comes his way. The results of projecting one's inner King onto others can be found in the loss of capacity to protect, provide and procreate. In other words, "we give up the joy of experiencing an integrated, autonomous sense of self."[53]

The challenge for men, therefore, is to develop a relationship with the full manifestation of archetypal energies, so as to not find themselves "possessed" by their shadows.[54]

The Warrior

Despite a societal repugnance toward violence, human history, socio-biology and depth psychology suggest that there is Warrior energy within the human species. In some quarters, Warrior energy has been repressed as "soft masculinity" and aggressive feminist critiques question its validity for the late twentieth century. In spite of such criticism, Moore/Gillette note that the Warrior archetype is an active part of the psyche, and to deny its place leads to the very forms of violence that it is supposed to oppose.

> We can't just take a vote and vote the Warrior out. Like all archetypes, it lives on in spite of our conscious attitudes toward it. And

like all *repressed* archetypes, it goes underground, eventually to resurface in the form of emotional and physical violence, like a volcano that has lain dormant for centuries with the pressure gradually building up in the magma chamber.[55]

The authors illustrate the positive effects of Warrior energy throughout history. They note that Warrior traditions are universal across time and tradition.[56] Accordingly, this is in part evidence of the influential presence of Warrior archetypes in the human epic.

> The Warrior energy, then, no matter what else it may be, is indeed universally present in us men and in the civilizations we create, defend, and extend. It is a vital ingredient in our world-building and plays an important role in extending the benefits of the highest human virtues and cultural achievements to all humanity.[57]

Warrior energy enables a man to have focus, clarity and absolute allegiance. If the King archetype illustrates the establishment of the boundaries of a man's psyche, then the Warrior archetype enforces and protects them. The Warrior archetype, when accessed, enables a man to live fully committed to a transpersonal other, instilling within him the capacity for commitment and purpose.

As with the King, the shadow side of the Warrior archetype is the image most common to contemporary popular imagination. Moore/Gillette contend that thoughtful people are in reaction, not to the archetype in its fullest expression, but to the effects of its Shadow manifestations. The Sadist and the Masochist, images of the Shadow Warrior, abound in men today.[58] In these opposite poles, men are driven to abusing others, or abusing themselves. Neither is a positive example of Warrior energy. In one pole, the Warrior turns outward in brutal exploitation. In the other, its disfiguring violence is turned inward.[59]

The positive expression of Warrior energy is found in men who are focused, dedicated, courageous, loyal, persevering and decisive. This ability to extend oneself comes from the gift of aggressiveness that the Warrior archetype brings. Popular self-help and management training textbooks shy away from the concept of aggressiveness, preferring instead assertiveness as the acceptable model of personal interaction. The Warrior archetype in its fullness demonstrates the positive value of aggressiveness. Moore/Gillette identify aggressiveness as "a stance toward life that rouses, energizes and motivates. It pushes us to take the offensive and to move out of a defensive or 'holding' position about life's tasks or problems."[60]

Warrior energy enables a man to avoid being swept away by fearful emotions when courage is needed. It provides men with the ability to undertake rigorous discipline and decisive action, and it frees men from the need to exact vengeance or to seek self-promotion. The Warrior, when leavened by the other three mature masculine archetypes, will produce men needed for the reconstructive efforts of society.[61]

The Magician

The Magician has been called the "compelling image of awareness, consciousness, growth and transformation."[62] The Magician archetype is that energy within a man which possesses a connection with the deep wisdom of the universe, and processes of transformation. Historically, the Magician was the keeper of secret knowledge. He ritually initiated others into that knowledge and offered his transformative power for the benefit of society. Anthropological studies have demonstrated that each society had its Magician: holy men, witch doctors, shamans, astrologers, seers, wizards, prophets all possessed the "great secrets" and, as such, held positions of power.[63] Modern manifestations of the Magician archetype can be found in "doctors, lawyers, priests, CEO's, plumbers and electricians, research scientists, psychologists."[64]

There are three characteristics common to the Magician archetype in its fullest expression. The Magician provides the capacity for profound reflection, analysis, insight and intellectual discovery. As is evident in the Hebrew scriptures, the prophets were able to see beyond the immediate socio-political reality and proclaim "The Word of the Lord." This "bullshit detector"[65] allows a man to discern beyond immediate appearance and exercise discriminating insight.

The second characteristic of the Magician is that of the transformer. The Magician enables a man to unite paradoxical experiences and seemingly create *ex nihilo*. The Magician archetype engages men in their quest for personal and societal transformation. It is the Magician that brings the "miraculous insight" into a perplexing question or problem which results in solutions. As Arnold notes, biblical literature illustrates the Magician in a number of instances. Chief for these reflections is the life of Jesus, where he accessed the Magician to change water into wine, to multiply loaves of bread and fish, to heal the sick, and to raise the dead to life.

The mythic interpretation of Jesus' life and ministry also points to the third characteristic of the Magician archetype—the Shaman. In traditional societies, the Shaman was the "healer, the one who restored life, the one who found lost souls and who discovered the hidden causes of misfortune."[66] In contemporary practice, this manifestation of the Magician informs the development of insight and technology for the good of society. The authors note:

> If we are accessing the Magician appropriately we will be adding to our professional and personal lives a dimension of clearsightedness, of deep understanding and reflection about ourselves and others, and technical skills in our outer nature and work and in our inner handling of psychological forces.[67]

The Lover

The Lover archetype creates and energizes the soul of a man, giving him an appetite for life.

We believe that the Lover, by whatever name, is the primal energy pattern of what we would call vividness, aliveness, and passion. It lives through the great primal hungers of our species for
sex, food, well-being, reproduction, creative adaptation to life's
hardships, and ultimately a sense of meaning, without which
human beings cannot go on with their lives.[68]

The Lover empowers men to delight in, to appreciate, and to
enjoy life. It humanizes men and provides them with the capacity to feel deeply. The Lover's energy is expressed in the poet, the
musician, the artist, the dancer. The Lover "sips the nectar of
life" and doesn't need to apologize for pleasure or joy. The Lover
is the archetype of play and of "display," of healthy embodiment,
of being in the world of sensuous pleasure and in one's own body
without shame.[69]

When a man accesses the Lover archetype, he encounters aesthetic consciousness, profound passion, deep feeling, sensuous
experience, and mystical ecstasy. Richard Rohr notes that the
mystic is the one who has accessed the Lover archetype. Mystics
are able to hold opposites together, by loving "what is" and participating in an experience of the unity of creation.[70] By participating in the deep experiences of life, the Lover leads men into
deep suffering as well.

There has been a tragic assault upon the Lover in most men's
lives. From early childhood, most men have experienced a sense
of shame about their sexuality, passion, and emotions.[71]
Contemporary culture places little value upon a man's ability to
be deeply connected to his emotive faculties. As noted in Chapter
1, the fashionable media icon is usually the strong, silent action
hero who "loves them and leaves them." The prevalent cultural
expression of the Lover is in its shadow manifestations: the
"Addicted Lover" and "Impotent Lover."[72] In either instance, the
Shadow-Lover objectifies the "other," and in doing so loses both
himself and the other.

The Lover guides men into the depth of emotional and soulful

living. The Lover empowers a man to care deeply about life in all
of its manifestations.

> The trouble with most of us is not that we feel too much passion,
> but that we don't feel our passion much at all. We don't feel our
> joy. We don't feel able to be alive and to live our lives the way we
> wanted to live them when we began.[73]

The discussion of connecting men to soul energy has come
full circle. A review of the tenets of archetypal psychology has
demonstrated that men experience the impact of archetypes
daily, seemingly unaware of their influence. The goal of men's
studies in relationship to archetypes is to teach men how to live
"fully, energetically, and creatively."[74] Moore/Gillette suggest
that this will occur as men learn how to access the archetypes
successfully.

> Analysis of dreams, the re-entering and changing of our dreams,
> active imagination (in which the Ego, among other things, dia-
> logues with the energy patterns within, thereby achieving both
> differentiation from and access to them), psychotherapy in a vari-
> ety of forms, meditation on the positive aspects of the archetypes,
> prayer, magical ritual process with a spiritual elder, various forms
> of spiritual discipline, and other methods are all important to the
> difficult process of turning boys into men.[75]

In masculine spirituality this quest becomes more focused.
Given the primacy of the doctrine of God's incarnation in the
human person, masculine spirituality seeks to understand archetypal energies as the movement of God within. In other words, it
is an attempt to understand the movement of God's spirit using
twentieth century paradigms. Richard Rohr characterizes this
spiritual vision of the archetypes:

> Archetypes are filled with generative power. They lead us into
> "sacred space" where we "see" for the first time. We understand,
> we know what we must do, and somehow in the fascination we

even find the energy to do it. When you are in the grip of an archetype, you have vision and a deep sense of meaning for your life....[76]

The Myths of a Man's Soul

As this chapter has shown, mythic consciousness informs masculine spirituality. The embodiment of archetypes into mythic images is an example of the symbolic universality of human nature. Masculine spirituality has great respect for the role of mythic story-telling, as it enables men to relate to their own unfolding journey. Joseph Campbell, the preeminent mythologist for this generation, notes:

> People say that what we're all seeking is a meaning for life. I don't think that's what we're really seeking. I think that what we're seeking is an experience of being alive, so that our life experiences on the purely physical plane will have resonances within our own innermost being and reality so that we actually feel the rapture of being alive.[77]

Myth is a particular way of explaining reality. It is different from the rational, linear and technical methods of western communication which have little room for symbol. As such it has been denigrated in the popular consciousness since the enlightenment.[78] Myth is not concerned with empirical fact in the way rational reflection is. Rather, myth seeks to experience great truth through saga and image. Stories of heroes, quests, dragons, knights, wildmen, maidens and angels speak to long dormant imaginative functions of men.

Religion and spirituality were formulated in mythic worlds. As such, their richness is diminished when mythology is denigrated.[79] Some authors suggest that the loss of the "poetic soul" within religion is partly responsible for the loss of a sense of the sacred. Campbell points to this when he says:

> Wherever myths are still living symbols, the mythologies are teeming dream worlds of such images. But wherever systematizing theologians have appeared and gained the day...the figures have become petrified into propositions.[80]

Masculine spirituality intentionally seeks to reclaim the mythic dimension of a man's consciousness by telling men ancient stories. This opens them to experience even further the soulful dimensions of their existence. There is a mythic-drivenness to men's work, and those who write on masculine spirituality are incorporating myth into their observations.

Three values for mythological reflection stand out in the development of a man's spirituality. First, mythology provides an explanation of seeming unexplainable reality. Quoting Heinrich Zimmer, Rohr notes, "The best things cannot be talked about. The second-best things are usually misunderstood."[81] Mythology, through the world of images, metaphors, symbols and story, allows a glimpse into patterns and rhythms of life that are shielded to contemporary consciousness. Patrick Arnold proposes:

> This is why we have myths. Some truths can't be told directly; they are too awful and too mysterious. So they are related covertly in stories that seem to be about people who lived long ago in faraway lands; actually they are about us.[82]

Second, mythological reflection enables a man to know that he is not alone on his quest for mature masculinity and God. Since mythology portrays the eternal and universal human struggle it becomes apparent that the development of the masculine spirit is not something unique to the individual. Communal reflection and initiation rites provide "mythical patterns of successful, heroic manhood from his family, religion and culture...."[83]

Third, myth opens a man to his own symbolic nature and provides interaction with his own depth. Richard Underwood suggests:

The true power of myth lies in its capacity to move one through and beyond so as to experience the Presence of Being. In the end, then, Campbell's understanding of the religious life-journey was an understanding that enables one to live *by* myth, not in myth.[84]

The Myths of Masculinity

There is a trilogy of popular masculine myths that are being used in masculine spirituality. In the first, "The Quest for the Holy Grail," several great patterns of masculine development are portrayed in the story of Parsifal. Richard Rohr has developed an exegetical synthesis of the twelfth century myth and has identified six movements in it to illustrate a man's quest for individuation and service: Separation and Departure, Early Preparation, The Grail Castle, The Deepening Spiral, Wandering/Avoidance/Denial, and the Return to the Castle. He has correlated these movements to necessary stages of masculine development. The great themes of the hero—"Separation, Encounter, and Return"—are all detailed in the myth.[85] Rohr notes:

In the myth, one is supposed to begin with naivete, then walk through the complexity and paradoxes of the labyrinth, and return at the end in second naivete. At the end point of the journey the hero is presented as the perfect fool, the holy fool, like St. Francis.[86]

In the second masculine myth, "Iron John,"[87] Robert Bly finds the necessary descent of a man into his instinctual energies. Imaginative moments, such as The Capture of the Wildman, The Loss of the Golden Ball, The Escape of the Wildman, The Wounded Boy with the Golden Hair, and The Divine Marriage, all typify shifts in the masculine consciousness from the feminine to the deep masculine. This instinctual energy in men has been long dormant, primarily due to a loss of "father energy" and masculine initiation.

Bly suggests that the loss of the relationship between father and son is the most traumatic effect of the industrial revolution. Prior to this, young boys worked with their fathers in the shop or on the farm. This side-by-side relationship allowed the man to impart masculine energy to his son, and this resulted in more psychically developed young men. With the advent of the father working away from the home, young men began to develop a "psychic hole" in which "demons began rushing in."[88] The myth of Iron John offers a man a path for escape from the bondage of the feminine…from the world of the "soft male."

The third masculine myth, "The White Snake," offers an alternative mythic view of masculine development. Philip Culbertson suggests that using mythic images such as "Iron John" to typify a man's development is not helpful for the post-modern age.

> We already know from the proper feminist critique of our inheritance what damage macho self-centeredness, conformity and anti-intellectualism can produce. Instead of seeking the wild man within, sensitive men should seek to nurture and to facilitate.[89]

Culbertson offers an alternate myth of a man's unfolding that stems from his vision of "sensitivity." This story of the White Snake evolves around a young man's encounters with The Wise King and the Secret Dish, The White Snake, The Song of the Animals, Friendship with Creation, The Princess and Apple of Life. Each of these movements within the myth corresponds to authentic virtues of masculine experience. Masculine virtues of docility, humility, adventurousness, and a valuation of creation are all imaged in mythic imagination in this story.

Summary

This chapter has been an attempt to introduce various reflections on the topic of men and soul. First, I've attempted to familiarize the reader with the various ways that "soul" is imaged in contemporary philosophical and theological reflections. This analysis demonstrated that there is a difference in the literature between a man's soul and his spirit.

Second, I reviewed the basic tenets of archetypal psychology as the context for appreciating the value that masculine spirituality places on the inner energy of the King, Warrior, Magician and Lover. I demonstrated the value of each archetype in the movement of masculine maturity.

Finally, I briefly introduced the use of mythology in masculine spirituality. Within the context of a review of the function and value of myth, I tried to show the merit of mythological reflection for the men's movement. It is clear that men must experience their own depths, and masculine spirituality will serve as a useful guide in that process insofar as it guides men on this quest.

4
The Integration of Masculine Spirituality

I have focused this book so far on theoretical assumptions underlying masculine spirituality. In Chapter 1, I presented some general conclusions about the "problem" of contemporary men. In Chapter 2, I reviewed questions that surround the discussion of gender based images of God. In Chapter 3, I examined issues of developing soul energy for men. In the remaining two chapters, I will examine the reflections of authors who are engaged in helping men identify the loss of masculine wholeness and find practical methods of restoring balance to their lives. This chapter will focus on authors who have reflected on the physical, psychic, sexual, spiritual, and/or relational alienation that men experience, and on authors who advocate practical ways of achieving masculine integration.

The Alienation of Men

The western male is in a state of alienation. Most men are alienated from themselves, their relationships, their environment, and ultimately their God. Reflecting upon the effects of the current crisis of masculinity, Sam Keen asks:

Why has the gender that gave us the Sistine Chapel brought us to the edge of cosmocide? Why have the best and brightest exercised their intelligence, imagination, and energy and managed only to create a world where starvation and warfare are more common than they were in neolithic times? Why has the history of what we dare to call "progress" been marked by an increase in the quantity of human suffering?[1]

As noted in Chapter 1, men experience deficits in personality development due to child rearing practices which tend to foster a boy's alienation from himself and others.[2] Men have been reared with a limited range of socially acceptable models of masculinity.[3] As such, a stunted and dominating masculine is a common expression of manhood for most in the west.[4] Such developmental defects become more evident when a boy grows up and enters the world of men. The symptoms of men's disconnection are socially manifest in increasing rates of male violence, delinquency, divorce and the abandonment of children. Statistics indicate that males overwhelmingly account for the majority of assault and homicide victims, persons with AIDS, and those homeless, or killed on the job.[5] The field of addictions research shows an abundance of data which point to men's disconnection from themselves. Jed Diamond, a licensed clinical social worker, notes:

> Untreated addictions continue to grow like cancer. Twenty-eight years ago, when I first began working in the field, men were dealing mostly with alcohol and heroin addictions. In recent years, there has been an addictions explosion. Men are now struggling with everything from homemade amphetamines to designer drugs, compulsive sex to destructive work, overspending to overeating.[6]

Many men suffer some significant degree of estrangement from relationships. Dwight H. Judy notes:

> There are problems for men in the area of aggression and violence and in a limited understanding of the potential for creative relationships with women in many diverse roles. We also find the male struggling with his relationships with men in authority and

with men as coequals in companionship. We find a negative view
of emotions and the human passions. We find men in many ways
cut off from others, as well as from their sources of both passionate energy and creative vision.[7]

Whether the divide is between a man and his own being, or a man
and others, most possess a limited capacity to engage in the challenges and satisfactions of relationships. Aaron Kipnis cites the
following as evidence of men's disconnection:

- Co-dependency
- Workaholism
- Emotional Numbness
- Addiction to Excitement
- Sexual Addictions
- Loss of Soul[8]

This inventory of masculine wounds resonates with many
authors writing in the field of masculine psychology/spirituality.
In his work, *The Intimate Connection*, James B. Nelson suggests
that men are wounded at the very essence of their masculinity.
These wounds result in an inability to embrace intimate relationships, friendships, or their own mortality.[9] Sam Keen labels the
post-modern man the "concupiscent consumer,"[10] who lives life
by aesthetic or sensual whim rather than from a moral or spiritual center. This betrays evidence of men's disconnection to their
own depths, as they make decisions based on fancy or feeling.

Those involved in the field of masculine psychology or spirituality agree that this fracture of the male psyche is evident in
men's addictions. Jed Diamond calls addictions the "disease of
lost self-hood…a loss of the primal connection with the masculine self."[11] He notes that through addictions men attempt to
substitute an attachment to a person, object or feeling for
authentic experiences of being—"of living life for its own
sake."[12] In recovery work, men unearth reservoirs of anger,
shame and despair that addictions previously masked. Diamond

suggests that addictions are often the result of attempts to deal with the pain of parental shaming or childhood abuse. In other words, "Our addictions became our way of dealing with our wounds."[13]

Diamond identifies alcohol, cocaine, narcotics, steroids, food, work, and money as the most common "masculine compulsions."[14] Attachment to any of these provides enough sensual stimulation to keep a man from being confronted with his emotional pain. He also notes that in addition to compulsive behavior, most men suffer from sex and love addictions, commonly called co-dependency.[15] Given men's inability to form authentic relationships, it is not surprising to discover that they look to others to provide them with feelings of acceptance, passion and significance. In a culture that places such a high value on sexuality, men have been socialized to view sexual activity as the chief means of receiving intimacy and tenderness. I will examine the issues of sexuality in greater detail later in this chapter. At this point, however, it is important to note that sexuality is a major source of addiction for men.

Diamond suggests that the study of addictions in men demonstrate that 1) all men are addicted to something or to someone; 2) recovery and restoration should begin sooner and continue longer than current practice dictates; 3) all addictions have a positive aspect that must be acknowledged; and 4) developing a mature masculine personality and recovering from addictive behavior are correlative tasks.[16]

There are a number of challenges necessary for men to address in their quest for wholeness. For the purpose of these reflections, I have categorized these challenges as "The Father Wound," "Warped Sexuality," and "Hatred of the Feminine." Each plays a crucial role in developing an authentic spirituality for men. Unless men successfully engage each of these challenges to psychological development, they will be forever alienated to some degree from God and others.

The Father Wound

As noted in Chapter 1, the relationship between father and son is perhaps the most ruptured relationship of our time. A popular notion of child rearing is that it is "the woman's responsibility." But the father is the boy's first significant non-maternal influence. One of the father's primary roles is to free a boy from his mother's influence. Jed Diamond notes:

> We need help in separating from the force field of the Woman or we will never make it to manhood. Her gravitational pull is too strong to resist on our own. Older males must be there to exert an even greater pull or we will always be afraid of being sucked back into our mother's orbit...we may grow physically, and do all the "manly" things, but inside we still feel like mama's boy.[17]

Consequently a father's responsibility is to assist his son in establishing a cohesive psychic structure. When this doesn't happen, the boy's ability to develop psychologically is hampered.

A memory common to many contemporary men is that their father was either absent or abusive. In men's gatherings there is little talk of the presence and support of the father. Instead, great sadness overtakes these groups as men speak about their unrealized hopes and dreams for relationships with their fathers. Robert Bly calls grief the "primary masculine emotion,"[18] based in large part upon his conversation with thousands of men still yearning for their father's love. In his work, *Iron John: A Book About Men*, Bly suggests that fathers need to pass on to their sons masculine energy, a "cellular knowledge." If this doesn't occur, then boys are unable to learn "at which frequency the masculine body emanates." He notes:

> Sons who have not received this retuning will have father-hunger all their lives. I think calling the longing "hunger" is accurate: the young man's body lacks salt, water, or protein, just as a starving person's body and lower digestive tract lack protein. If it finds none, the stomach will eventually eat up the muscles themselves.

Such hungry young men hang around older men like the homeless do around a soup kitchen. Like the homeless, they feel shame over their condition, and it is nameless, bitter, unexpungeable shame.[19]

In his book, *Absent Fathers, Lost Sons*, Guy Corneau reflects upon the consequence of the father's absence. He notes that the crisis of absent fathers is reaching epidemic proportions. In 1988, one in five children lived in a fatherless home and eighty-nine percent of these homes were headed by women.[20] Even when a man lives in the home, Corneau suggests that there is no guarantee of effective fathering:

The term absent fathers...refers to both the psychological and physical absence of fathers and implies both spiritual and emotional absence. It also suggests the notion of fathers who, although physically present, behave in ways that are unacceptable: authoritarian fathers, for example, are oppressive and jealous of their sons' talents and smother their sons' attempts at creativity or self-affirmation. Alcoholic fathers' emotional instability keeps their sons in a permanent state of insecurity.[21]

Corneau notes that when a breach exists between a father and his son, the child is at a loss for a means of establishing his own masculine identity and is "unable to advance to adulthood."[22] Violence, should it occur, intensifies this fracture, and the boy's identity becomes even more fragile. Corneau suggests that the father plays the following developmental tasks in the life of his son:

- The father teaches his son how to become independent from his mother.
- The father makes it possible for his son to develop his own capacity for self-affirmation and self-defense.
- The father provides his son with the psychic safety to develop his sense of exploration, sexuality, and independence.
- The father encourages his son's achievements and teaches him responsibility.[23]

He submits that fathers vitiate the necessary link to masculine energy when they are absent for a prolonged period of time, neglect their son's need for affection, threaten to abandon him, shame or cling to him.[24] This is often evidenced when a father demands that his son "follow in his footsteps" or be successful in ways that the father couldn't. This type of abusive behavior creates a son who lacks self-confidence, has adjustment disorders, is "given to anxieties, depression, obsessions, compulsions and phobias."[25] Corneau notes that a boy who has experienced such paternal neglect struggles with sexual identity, represses aggression, lacks healthy ambition, suffers from learning disorders, has a diminished sense of moral value and personal responsibility, and often turns to some form of substance abuse in an attempt to quench his inner psychic turmoil.[26] Patrick Arnold notes that "psychologists and counselors tell us that many American men bear these father-wounds all their lives, never understanding them much less finding healing with their fathers."[27] To summarize the depths of the problem, Corneau writes:

> The father's absence results in the child's lack of internal structure....His ideas are confused; he has trouble setting himself goals, making choices, deciding what is good for him, and identifying his own needs. For him, everything gets mixed up: love and reason, sexual appetites and the simple need for affection. He sometimes has problems concentrating, he is distracted by all sorts of insignificant details....Basically he never feels sure about anything.[28]

One of the deleterious effects of the father wound is the effect that it has on society at large. As noted previously, sociologists indicate that a disproportionate number of delinquent boys come from homes where the father was either absent or abusive. In order to compensate for a lack of healthy male energy or role models, boys become hyper-masculine and violent. Male violence is then perpetuated upon other men, women, children, and animals and ultimately the environment. This cycle of violence continues to the next generation as the latest batch of wounded men produce alienated sons, who in turn do the same to their sons. This poisonous pedagogy is self-perpetuating unless something breaks the effects of this abusive chain.[29]

To summarize, the lack of effective fathering is one of the most profound deficits that a boy can experience. A review of the literature demonstrates that boys who experience either abusive or absent fathers lack the ability to develop coherent psychic structures. This deficiency leads to a host of psychological, relational, sexual and spiritual challenges that boys are unable to meet. This type of fathering (or lack of it) is perpetuated generationally, and the damage to the corporate masculine psyche is evident in the addictions, compulsions and disorders noted above.

Warped Sexuality

Patrick Arnold asserts that "sexuality gives our personal as well as our faith relationships depth, color, excitement, and vivacity."[30] Counselors tell us that one of the disastrous effects of the "father wound" is the warping of a boy's sexual identity. Those who work with men don't need statistics to understand that male sexuality is in trouble. What was designed by God as a gift and means of life has become a source of deep pain for men. Many men have little understanding of the difference between sex and love, intimacy and intercourse. The richness of a man's sexuality is usually shrouded in ignorance, fear and despair. Men know that something is missing, but the socialization of young men creates more questions than answers. Until the last thirty years, boys were not offered any formal education in sexual matters, and today's contemporary sexual pedagogy tends toward a mechanical view of sexual activity. Accordingly, those authors who work with men indicate that confusion and shame are two pervasive wounds to a man's sexuality.

James B. Nelson's book, *The Intimate Connection*, offers helpful reflections in the domain of masculine sexuality and spirituality. Nelson notes that the Christian faith holds that sexuality is a constitutive part of a man.[31] A man's sexuality is one way that God expresses incarnational love and presence in the world. According to Nelson, Christianity inspires a belief that sexuality is about more than a physical act leading to ejaculation and orgasm. Rather, it views sexuality as a part of a person's constitutive psychic makeup which leads to expressions of vulnerability, passion, love and connection.[32]

A review of the contemporary sexual landscape reveals a far different picture. Sex for the sake of sex is commonplace, as are the plethora of diseases and disorders that accompany it. Movies and television shows portray little relationship between love, commitment, vulnerability and sex. Instead, messages of recreational sexual activity are commonplace in the entertainment industry. Pornography is no longer restricted to seedy movie theaters on the edge of town. The sale and rental of pornographic home video is a multi-billion dollar industry in America in the 1990s. Steven Hill notes:

> In the United States, 22 million men spend $2 billion a year on a range of 105 pornographic magazines. Porn films gross $5 million per day and the porn industry earns over-the-counter profits of $8 billion per year.[33]

To the extent that this distorted and commercialized view of sex dominates the cultural landscape, it robs men of the power and beauty of their sexuality.

A particular mythology of sexuality has developed, and men are seemingly driven to live the myth. Don Sabo submits that the common masculine mythology for sex revolves around men as the "sexual athlete." This myth views sex as a sport, has its own language, involves score-keeping and conquest, and is oriented toward performance and reward.[34] Sam Keen identifies two predominant roles of men within the sexual myth. Men are expected to 1) fulfill the role of the "sexual warrior"—to conquer and possess as many women as possible as a proof of his potency, and

2) to fulfill the role of the "sexual worker," to "make love, perform, to produce the intended result—satisfying the woman."[35] This banal sexual mythology objectifies both parties. The love, commitment and appreciation of the "other" has no place in contemporary sexual expression. The sex partner, whether a woman, another man, a child, or an animal, become a means for personal gratification. Beauty, dignity, and intimacy are lost as performance, success, prestige, anger, fear and power become the common denominators in men's sexual experience.

The effect of the current sexual pedagogy is devastating to the psychic and moral health of young men. Men experience a dualistic split as they feel driven to sexual experience, and yet react to prevailing cultural mores and trends. Depending on the cultural voices that a man chooses to listen to, sexuality is either celebrated or condemned. He is encouraged to "score" as often as he can, or he is instructed that he must remain chaste in anticipation of his honeymoon. This denies the vast middle ground of sexuality. First, it reinforces a dualistic notion that a man's body is separate from his soul and spirit. Second, it limits sexuality to mechanical action alone. Third, it keeps the focus of sexual expression in the realms of either performance or gratification. Finally, it keeps a man's sexuality wrapped within a mantle of shame.[36]

Several authors note that a man's sexual shaming begins very early in life and continues throughout adolescence. Wounding the sexual organ at birth, such as through circumcision, inaugurates the shaming process.[37] As the boy matures he is told in subtle ways that his body is "dirty" and animal, and that his sexual urges and desires are to be avoided at all costs. Philip Culbertson notes:

> In reality, many men experience conflict about sex, partly due to the double message we learned as children: sex is dirty, and sex should be saved for someone you love. In other words, spend your youth accumulating the worst dose of self-loathing and

repression you can think of, and then dump it on the most special person in your life.[38]

The degree to which sexuality is a source of shame is evidenced by society's preoccupation with it. As noted above, boys are routinely socialized toward either blatant promiscuity or repressed chastity. Sigmund Freud once noted that a person's denials tell as much about the person as do one's affirmations. The vast amount of money and energy spent demonizing or defending sexuality in our culture is indicative of the inordinate social fixation upon sexuality. Rather than being celebrated as a gift of God given to enhance and enrich life, sex has become a source of great pain for men.

The shame that men experience about their sexuality is multiplied when it comes to homosexual men. Centuries of prejudice and oppression have convinced many gay men that they are flawed at the essence of their being. This results in an ever downward spiral of shame as they struggle with the same need that every man has: for love, tenderness, erotic interaction and intimacy. Daniel Helminiak notes, "Much human potential is squashed and wasted in people who live for years in secret self-hatred, taught to be afraid of their own hearts."[39] He observes the results of societal intolerance of homosexuality:

- Thirty to forty percent of children living on the streets were thrown out or left their homes because they are homosexual.

- Thirty percent of teenage suicides, two to three times higher than the national norm, are among homosexual youth.

- The employment status of homosexual people is at risk when their orientation becomes known.

- Homosexual parents lose custody of their children, are evicted from their homes, are routinely beaten up or murdered, and in some instances are denied adequate medical care and die alone: all due to the inability of society to tolerate their presence.[40]

In light of ever expanding evidence about the nature of psycho-sexual orientation,[41] the damage that heterosexism generates takes on a more sinister character. "Gay bashing" is at an all time high as men, afraid of the implications of homosexuality, resort to violence and, in some cases, murder to stamp out its "plague."

This brief review demonstrates some aspects of the warped sexuality that contemporary men experience. Whether gay or straight, men live with confusion and shame relative to their sexuality. A review of the literature available on this topic demonstrates that an underdeveloped sexuality inhibits men's ability to love themselves, others or God.[42] Rather than having companions, lovers or spouses, men look for sex objects to satisfy cravings for intimacy, tenderness or passion.

Hatred of the Feminine

"Women, you can't live with them and you can't live without them," or so says traditional masculine lore. Women remain a source of constant fascination for men. The woman is the one where men first reside in amniotic bliss, she is the one who brings men into the world, and she is the first one to whom men look for nourishment and life. To some degree, men never separate from the world of women. In contemporary culture this assessment seems ever more apt, as there are fewer older men walking boys through initiation rituals designed to break the hold of the woman upon the man. Men remain under WOMAN's spell for most of their lives. Keen writes:

> It was slow in dawning on me that WOMAN had an overwhelming influence on my life and on the lives of all the men I knew. I am not talking about women, the actual flesh-and-blood creatures, but about WOMEN, those larger-than-life shadowy female

figures who inhabit our imaginations, inform our emotions, and indirectly give shape to many of our actions.[43]

An abundance of multi-disciplinary literature indicates that young boys must differentiate not only physically from the feminine, but psychologically as well. As noted above, one of the most devastating results of the "father wound" is that men remain trapped in the control of the feminine, unable to rescue themselves. Anthropologists and mythologists propose that tribal initiatory rituals were designed to facilitate the differentiation process for boys. Robert Bly notes:

> When initiation is in place, the old men help the boys to move from the mother's world to the father's world. Boys have lived happily since birth in the mother's world, and the father's world naturally seems to them dangerous, unsteady, and full of unknowns. We recall that most cultures describe the first stage of initiation as a clean and sharp break with the mother. Old men simply go into the women's compound one day with spears when the boys are between eight and twelve and take the boys away.[44]

Many authors posit that since older men have abdicated their responsibility as initiators, younger men have not been effectively introduced to hearty masculine ways of knowing and loving. As a result, men remain in bondage to WOMAN. When one is struggling to break free from WOMAN, one cannot respect, honor and love women. Psychologists note that an inability to separate from WOMAN results in a bondage which enslaves a man to the feminine. This terrifying servitude has many faces to it. Men worship women, while abusing them. They entice women, charm them, sometimes even purchase them, all the while experiencing fear and anxiety about their relationship to them. This fear is not limited to women, but also to a man's own latent feminine characteristics. Philip Culbertson writes of the "fear of the feminine":

> Many men have been taught to shun whatever smacks of "playing the woman's role," for they do not know how to define mas-

culinity other than be a sequence of "nots": not feminine, not womanly, not passive-receptive, not soft, not "on the bottom."[45]

This fear of the feminine is not limited to heterosexual men. In some facets of the gay community there tends to be a misogynist paradigm, where women are spurned, not only as sexual partners, but as friends, confidantes, and sisters in faith. Regardless of psycho-sexual orientation, the fear or hatred of the feminine is a consequence of a man's inability to integrate psychologically.

In his book, *He: Understanding Masculine Psychology*, Robert Johnson points to the tragic results of a man's failure to differentiate between the different parts of his own psyche. When he is unable to integrate the feminine elements of his own psyche, a man projects his feminine presence into the outer world, onto flesh and blood women. Patrick Arnold notes:

Many men are completely unaware that the "ideal woman"—soft, gentle, and mysterious—that they can never find, or sweeps them off their feet when they do, is within themselves. The only kind of women "out there" in the real world are real, flesh-and-blood women.[46]

This projection will be either highly positive or extremely negative, but never neutral. In other words, men expect women to provide what they are unable to: men expect women to feel for them, to provide them with comfort and nourishment, softness and empathy, to demonstrate depth of feeling and animation.[47]

This projection explains men's bondage to WOMAN. A man cannot live without a connection to the inner and outer feminine.[48] To compensate, women are objectified and, hence, controlled by men, both gay and straight. Women become queens or whores, goddesses or servants, all in an attempt to maintain some sense of distance and mastery over them.

To summarize, feminists have long pointed to the dangers of men's inability to co-exist with the feminine. Historically men have viewed women as their property, as objects of their sexual fantasies, and as servants who perform a variety of tasks upon demand. Psychological theory has demonstrated that this is primarily due to a man's fear and hatred of all that is feminine within himself. This fear and hatred is projected onto flesh and blood women who unnecessarily bear the burden and violence of men.

Mature Masculinity

A formidable challenge exists for the men's movement as it seeks to guide men through processes of integration and recovery. As noted above, recovery work for men necessarily involves healing the personal, relational and environmental facets of a man's life. There are a number of authors who have identified a series of tasks that men must undertake if they hope to heal the split in their lives and relationships. Aaron Kipnis has identified the following tasks which heal the masculine soul.

- To admit woundedness.
- Begin healing by examining wounds.
- Rebuild self-esteem on deep masculine foundations.
- Break out of old stereotypes and claim diversity.
- Reclaim ancient sacred images of masculinity.
- Apply the myths of masculine soul to daily living.
- Rediscover male initiation and heal wounds between father and son.
- Love and work in ways that heal the masculine life.
- Restore connecting with ancestors and come to terms with mortality.
- Build male community and begin healing wounds between sexes.
- Develop a masculine affirming psychology.
- Continue reawakening the masculine soul.[49]

Kipnis is not alone in appreciating the value of formational tasks for men. Sam Keen suggests that there are ten movements toward maturity,[50] Dwight Judy identifies five goals for the quest of male healing,[51] and Philip Culbertson proposes a threefold agenda for masculine development.[52]

While other authors might vary their approach, the consensus of the literature is that men must intentionally participate in this journey of growth and integration. Men must first examine the roots of their ambivalence and hostility toward themselves and others. Next, they need to recognize flawed parental influences and stereotypical patterns of masculinity, and then break free from them. Finally, men must explore and embody new models of masculinity and manly living.

In his work, *The Warrior's Journey Home: Healing Men, Healing the Planet*, Jed Diamond offers a helpful model for men's healing and integration. Diamond's "Ten Tasks of the Mature Masculine" resonate with the other models of development noted above. For the purposes of these reflections, a brief review of Diamond's work will provide practical insight into the healing process for men. To summarize the work, Diamond suggests that men must:

1) Balance the desire to "do" with the need to "be." Men are socialized in ways that are oriented toward action and accomplishment. For authentic growth to occur, Diamond suggests that men must heal the rift in their psyche that values action over essence, doing over being.[53]

2) Understand and heal confusions about sex and love. Men have a distorted view of sexuality and love. As noted above, physical sexual expression is often the only way that men have been taught to "feel love." Mature masculine development points men toward "understanding, accepting, and integrating sex and love."[54]

3) Transform ambivalent feelings toward women and children. Men experience a love/hate relationship toward women and children. This ambivalence is often rooted in unresolved psychic and emotional conflict. Any effort toward masculine wholeness must address these sources of conflict and teach men how to appreciate women and children as individuals in their own right and not as property of men.[55]

4) Express grief over the absence of the father and risk getting close to other men. As previously noted, the absence of the father leaves deep wounds in many men. This lack of a strong, centered masculine presence inhibits a man's ability to develop relationships with other men. Men's work necessarily involves walking men through the grief of the "Father Wound" and teaching men how to form relationships that are rooted in mutuality, and not in competition.[56]

5) Change self-hatred to self-actualization. Given the lack of wholesome male role models, it is commonplace for men to develop an insecure personality which leads to self-loathing. Masculine development offers men the ability to relinquish self-hatred and to learn expressions of self-love and care.[57]

6) Acknowledge wounds and heal body and soul. In a society that seems to be focused on the physical beauty of women, it comes as a surprise that men are often ashamed of their bodies. "Shame, in all its various forms, manifests itself on a physical level."[58] Accordingly, if a man is ashamed of his body, he will not likely care for it. The task of the man is to acknowledge his wounds, provide better self-care and move toward a more healthy lifestyle.[59]

7) Uncover the basic roots of insecurity. The separation that men experience in the physical world is evidence of their insecurity within their psychic world. Men today experience little connection to a place, a tribe, or a culture. As such, they must learn to develop a communitarian ethic which provides a safe environment in which to grow.[60]

8) Acknowledge and heal hidden childhood abuse. As noted above, many current disciplinary practices of parents are abusive at their core. Parental violence, whether physical or verbal, is a commonplace experience for many boys. The invitation of mature masculinity is to recognize the historical evidence of childhood abuse and heal the wounds that abuse left behind.[61]

9) Explore the origins of violence and change destructive behavior. The socialization of men often encourages the use of violence as an effective means of conflict resolution. Diamond notes that the rage that is present in many men makes masculine ferocity commonplace. Authentic growth calls for an analysis and repudiation of the way that men were trained to rely first on violence, and then to change the way that boys resolve conflict.[62]

10) Return to the spirit of true warriors. Anthropological studies indicate that for the majority of human history men lived as a hunter-gatherer, that is, in partnership with the earth. It has only been in most recent history that men have lost the ability to act as a "Sacred Warrior," one who has great respect for every facet of life. Diamond suggests that men now live as "dominators," viewing creation as a commodity for their consumption. He suggests that returning to the spirit of the sacred warrior and achieving mature masculine self-esteem are correlative tasks.[63]

This review demonstrates a possible direction for men to take in their quest for wholeness and integration. The strength of these models is their holistic approach to the developmental process. Rather than focusing only on alleviating addictive relationships or compulsive behaviors, these developmental tasks encourage a lifelong process of becoming a mature masculine personality.

Masculine Spirituality and the Via Positiva

Christian spirituality is specifically concerned with humankind's relationship with God. As such, it takes seriously the full spectrum of ways that men and women encounter God. In this light, masculine spirituality is attentive to the "God path" for men. Masculine spirituality is concerned with every aspect of a man's life—his prayers, emotions, body, and relationships. As noted in the beginning of this chapter, the development of a healthy spirituality depends on the degree to which they are able to participate in the process of integration called for in these pages.

While masculine spirituality affirms the value of the developmental or formational tasks of the authors noted above, it also recognizes that they don't answer the question of how to integrate spirituality and a man's life. Each of these authors illustrates necessary steps for men to take toward integration and healing, but they don't address the central question of this work: How does masculine spirituality participate in the integration of a man? The remainder of this chapter seeks to address that question.

Dwight H. Judy proposes that spiritual practices and philosophies of the past are counter-productive in the quest to heal contemporary men because they dismiss much of the human personality. He notes that the development of Christian practice has been rooted in paradigms that are decidedly opposed to the experience of passion, emotion and embodiment. While Christianity seeks to provide spiritual practices which enliven its adherents, the ascetic and purgative style of monasticism seems to be idealized. As an example of this thought, Judy recognizes:

> The aim of the spiritual life was to become transformed within this body. One of the primary gauges of this transformation process was the degree to which the passions ceased to trouble one. The underlying assumption is that one cannot attain the insights of the spiritual realm while also being involved in the body's passions. Passionlessness is a goal for spiritual growth.[64]

Judy suggests that, historically, the goal of western spirituality has been one of "purity of heart, involving a perfection of emotions as well as of actions."[65] This *via negativa*, or way of purgation, viewed emotionality and physicality with suspicion. He notes that there are three harmful assumptions that emerge from the *via negativa*. The first implication that emerges from this type of spiritual practice is that it distrusts human emotion. Contrary to sound psychological evidence, this spirituality holds that the emotions are somehow tainted by the influence of sin and untrustworthy. Second, the *via negativa* has a negative perception of the physical world. Creation has become warped through

"Adam's fall," and, as such, has limited value. This warped view of creation legitimates the consumeristic attitude that has developed in western culture. Third, the *via negativa* enshrines mental practice over physical awareness as the most reliable source of interaction with God.[66]

Judy appreciates the solid emphasis on discipline and cognitive practice, but he calls for the development of a paradigm of spiritual practice which heals the male soul. Building upon the creation spirituality of Matthew Fox,[67] Judy labels this emerging spirituality as the *via positiva*. This *via positiva* celebrates every dimension of a man's life and experience as conduits of relationship with an incarnational God. This *via positiva* is a resolution of the ancient split between matter and spirit. In other words, "If God truly is flesh, then through flesh one finds God."[68] Practically, the *via positiva* suggests that the intersection between God and man occurs in the realm of emotion, passion, body and psyche.

There are three implications that spring from this position. First, the *via positiva* recognizes the value of human emotions. Instead of devising methods to quash the presence of a man's emotional life, he is encouraged to "listen" to those emotions for traces of God's connection. Second, creation and the physical world are highly valued in the *via positiva*. Creation is good and there is a vibrant presence of God to be discovered there. Accordingly, "matter" or things human have an intrinsic value to them and can be a locus of God's presence. Third, the *via positiva* encourages a man's physical awareness as a complementary partner to the development of the cognitive faculty. God speaks through the mind, but God also speaks through somatic awareness, emotional reactions and sensual passions.

As noted above, the *via positiva* is highly incarnational in its orientation. It celebrates God's divinizing presence in the world, in men and in women. When God "became flesh" in Jesus Christ, the evolution of spiritual consciousness reached a new level of awareness and possibility.[69] This increased awareness embraces universal experiences of wisdom and insight as legitimate disclosures of God's presence and love for humankind.

This is not to suggest that the *via positiva* is a spiritual practice given to physical excess. It is a call to restore a proper balance between all created energies within the human person. For most men, it is an invitation to befriend instinctual and passionate energies that have been repressed in the name of a "perfect spiritual life." It is a quest of discovering God through movements into their own personality. This pilgrimage recognizes the value of boundaries, of common morality, and of the primacy of love. But it asks men to reconnect with dimensions of their own being where God has long been waiting to embrace them. Judy reflects on this process:

> A primary path for me in coming to know my soul has been the body. Learning to live with the energies of the body, particularly its lower passions: sexual and aggressive....What wholeness required of me was to come into contact with the warrior energies....In liberating these lower energies, however, the higher energies have also awakened: the energies of the spiritual radiance as well as direct communion with the inner Christ.[70]

The *via positiva* is a path of both spiritual and psychological liberation and integration. All the sound psychological practices identified in these pages can be direct experiences of a healing quest into the love of God. Men can develop integrated and holistic personalities knowing that such freedom is a gift of God.

Men can grieve the loss of their fathers and experience the love of God through self-parenting and the reparenting of other men.[71] Instead of living with body-shame, men can participate in prayerful exercises designed to heal the distortions of the body image.[72] Rather than experiencing confusion, addiction and shame about sexuality, men can come to know that "sexuality is intrinsic to the divine-human experience."[73] Gay men can learn that an authentic Christian life is possible because "masculinity is not about whom you sleep with; it is about who you are and who you wish to become...it is about becoming your own man and following your bliss."[74] Men can come to know women for the actual people that they are, rather than remain entranced by undifferentiated psychological forces. They can tap into their own feminine essence and discover creativity, passion, sensitivity and tenderness.[75] In other words, they can learn to love *SOPHIA* within them.[76]

Finally, Judy suggests that through the practice of the *via positiva* men can learn to appreciate their strengths and gifts, not in opposition to the desire of others, but rather as an expression of their own fullness in relationship to God. "Stand up, take on your full capacity as a man, the capacity for power, the capacity for vision, and then God will address you face to face."[77]

Summary

The aim of this chapter has been to demonstrate the disconnection that characterizes contemporary men. First, I examined the symptoms of men's alienation from themselves and others: co-dependency, workaholism, emotional numbness, addictions, violence and anger. Then I examined the "Father Wound," "Warped Sexuality," and a "Hatred of the Feminine" as challenges to a man's physical, emotional and spiritual well-being. Next, I surveyed the work of various authors engaged in leading men through a quest for wholeness. I identified some of the tasks that men must undertake if they are to move into mature masculinity. Finally, I sketched a *via positiva* for masculine spirituality. There I showed that such a spiritual practice could lead contemporary men into an encounter with God by physical, emotional and psychological awareness. It is not an understatement to suggest that men need to undertake the journey of healing and integration for themselves, for others, for the world, and for their relationship with their God.

5
The Community of Man

In Chapter 4, I outlined some fundamental challenges that men need to undertake to move toward reintegration and a mature masculine personality. But as long as men remain isolated from others, any of the paths, disciplines, or techniques reviewed in this book will have limited value. Masculine spirituality is concerned with men's ability to experience life-giving relationships with God and others. As such it places great value on gatherings of men which foster intimacy and community among men.

This chapter will focus on the power of intentional gatherings of men to facilitate and experience vulnerability, trust and communion. First, I will examine the reflections of several authors who value communally based masculinity. These reflections will offer a review of the practical ways that men gather together for growth and support: discussion groups, drumming circles, lodges, etc. Next, I will treat the development and value of initiation rites as practiced in men's groups. Several authors are trying to reimagine ways that boys might be initiated into a lifestyle of authentic masculinity, and their reflections will be considered. Finally, I will present a vision of authentic masculinity that charts a path for men to follow in their quest for an authentic spirituality.

"No man," as the poem says, "is an island." Yet, an examination of the contemporary masculine landscape reveals a far different picture. An image common to masculine consciousness is one of man-as-solitary-hero. Whether on the athletic field, in the corporate boardroom, or within the family, men are socialized toward individual achievement and away from communitarian commitment. As Aaron Kipnis notes,

> Although many cultures have very different ideals concerning masculinity, in our culture the hero is one of the more prominent figures. We all grew up on John Wayne, whose basic image was that of a loner who defeats the bad guys against impossible odds and saves the lady in distress.[1]

After cataloging a long list of cultural icons who fit this model, he concludes that "the entrepreneur, the lone financier/magnate, has become a prominent heroic ideal in our culture."[2] Competition and independence are enshrined as preeminent values of any society which esteems the hero. Boys are encouraged to aspire toward rugged individualism, and cooperation is appreciated insofar as it advances some type of team endeavor. Even within the context of team effort, be it athletic or corporate, competition aimed at becoming "number one" is still the purpose of accomplishment. Mutuality is disdained and individual achievement, usually at great personal cost, becomes the celebrated goal for men. Patrick Arnold calls this attitude an "evil spirit that needs an exorcism."[3] Robert Bly offers a look into the results of this mindset when he writes:

> Contemporary business life allows competitive relationships only in which the major emotions are anxiety, tension, loneliness, rivalry, and fear. After work what do men do? Collect in a bar to hold light conversations over light beer, unities which are broken off whenever a young woman comes by or touches the brim of some cowboy hat. Having no soul union with men is the most damaging wound of all.[4]

As demonstrated in Chapter 2, the masculine capacity for

focused endeavor has produced many beneficial results for humankind. The eradication of disease, the building of complex disaster relief efforts, and athletic performance of Olympian proportions testify to men's capacity for accomplishment. Sadly, the shadow side of accomplishment is the tendency toward individualism, competition and achievement. This paradigm serves to keep men isolated from others. In a dog-eat-dog world, there is precious little room for interaction, interdependence and communion. Loneliness and isolation are a common way of life for many men. Conventional masculine socialization is oriented at best around a goal or task, or, at worst, rooted in shallow diversion.[5] Rather than provide men with the opportunity to experience new dimensions of masculinity, most fraternal gatherings allow men to run as far away from them as possible.

This work has highlighted the effects of child rearing practices which alienate a boy from both his environment and his relationships. Recall that boys are socialized in a different manner than girls. They are expected to move away from the nuclear family in both attitude and practice more rapidly than girls. In men's gatherings, conversation often revolves around the isolation that they experienced as boys. They lament the fact that they were expected to grow up too fast, to be "little men" before they were ready. Boys are raised with the expectation that they will be tougher than girls, will disregard pain, will ignore their emotions or needs, and are "pushed into assertive, aggressive, and nondependent behavior."[6]

Jed Diamond notes that these socialization practices produce four shame-based "core beliefs" which reinforce a man's isolation from others. After years of working with men he has observed that many have internalized these messages and interpret all of their experience through them:

- I am damaged and therefore bad inside.
- To know me is to abuse me or abandon me.
- If I have to rely on people to meet my needs, I will die.

• I must fill up the emptiness inside me by more (sex, drugs, alcohol, money, etc.).[7]

Given the ways that many boys are reared in western culture, the degree of isolation men experience should come as no surprise. The ranks of the "walking wounded" are filled with men who have had essential parts of their psychic and emotional lives severed from consciousness.

Every Man Needs a Lodge

Support groups have long been noted as an effective avenue for people to open themselves to new experiences of relating, of risking vulnerable disclosure, of receiving critique and challenge, and of learning to receive love and to care for others. Group sessions have been part of the therapeutic milieu for some time. Support groups, typified by the various "twelve-step" programs, have gained popularity as they lead people away from patterns of isolation and into communal methods of relationship. Gender-specific support groups are increasing in popularity as people seek to understand and relate in new ways, both masculine and feminine.

Men are gathering more frequently to explore issues of authentic masculine identity and to challenge sociological paradigms that are out-of-date. Sam Keen makes this observation:

In one sense the voyage of self-discovery is solitary, but that doesn't mean you have to take it all alone. A lot of men suffer silently when they are in creative chaos, and feel something is wrong with them because they don't realize other men are experiencing a similar disintegration of the old modes of masculinity. In matters of the psyche and spirit, taking the journey and telling the story go hand in glove, and that is why we need a listening community in order to make our solitary pilgrimage.[8]

Some view men's gatherings as a relatively new sociological phenomenon. However, anthropological research indicates that men have gathered together for generations to "perform sacred rites and delve into male mysteries."[9] These circles may have a specific focus for gathering. A review of men's journals indicates that men grapple with such issues as legal rights and responsibilities, consciousness raising, native-American spirituality, co-dependency and relationships, recovery from addictions, gay rights, and masculine mythology and ritual action. Other groups are formed so that its participants, aware of their relational deficits, can learn how to trust and befriend other men. Regardless of design, these "questing communities"[10] characteristically invite men into unfamiliar dimensions of "friendship, community and intimacy."[11] It is in these settings that the "evil spirit" of competition and independence alluded to by Patrick Arnold can be "exorcised."[12] Kipnis comments upon his own experience of men's groups:

> The new knights don't have any special chemistry or magic. We're not particularly brave, smart, cool, or lucky. We're essentially ordinary men who took the risk of reaching out to one another. We asked each other for help and offered it in return. We didn't pay anyone to be our expert healer. We just took turns. Fools and wise men all, stumbling along through the dark, being steadfast companions to one another in the quest of masculine soul.[13]

It is important to recognize that the nature of these new men's groups is dissimilar to fraternal associations of the previous generation. Arnold recalls that in the past, most have been little more than a "raucous Monday Night Football contingent or a faithful cadre whose main purpose is to organize the annual spring grounds clean-up."[14] Kipnis suggests that groups such as the Elks or Moose Lodge are historically rooted in philanthropic and social activities, but pay little attention to the issues of men's souls.[15] Jerome Bernstein recognizes the same:

> Many of those male groups that do remain intact have lost their purpose. They no longer serve as secret societies where mascu-

line mysteries are shared and learned. Many have denigrated into hiding places where men gather to socialize as they hide from the Devouring Mother.[16]

The reflections of authors who work with men indicate that these intentional gatherings are not only a place of fellowship and learning but also a sanctuary where masculine healing occurs. Paramount among the ways that men are healed in these settings is that they begin to talk, to express the torrent of emotion, fear and wonder that has been quarantined within them. As Kipnis has observed:

Talking about our personal issues—our hopes, fears, frustrations, and weaknesses—is more difficult. Expressing our uncensored feelings to one another is even more challenging. But it's more healing, valuable, and a better use of the limited time we have available for men's work. Through revealing our wounds, we also engender support for whatever crisis or difficulty we are experiencing at the moment.[17]

At their essence, these groups exist to break down walls that separate men from other men. Four characteristics of men's groups facilitate this process of awareness and reunion. First, in the safety of these gatherings, men experience the depth of their loneliness, grief, fear and confusion.[18] Men's groups provide the support and intimacy that allow men to unearth long repressed emotions. It is common for men engaged in this process to connect with feelings that were repressed from consciousness. Second, men are drawn away from societal and self-imposed isolation. In these groups, they recognize that others battle similar demons, wrestle with similar questions, and that they are not alone in their journey. As they talk with and listen to other men, they discover the deficits of parental and cultural assumptions, and learn that there are alternative ways of thinking and relating available.[19]

Third, men begin to experience the validation of their particular emotional needs. Kipnis suggests that one of the values of men's groups is that they expose men to the differences in the ways that they experience their emotions and discover that "men have a different emotional language and mode of expression than women."[20] As such, these groups provide a forum for men to explore their emotional dimensions and to understand that there are ways of caring for others that are uniquely masculine. Fourth, men's gatherings provide opportunities to experience the touch of men in ways that are not violent or sexual.[21] Authors such as Diamond, Kipnis, Rohr and Keene recognize that men have little capacity to relate intimately to other men. Rooted in both a distrust of the body and prevailing heterosexist ideologies, men often "seize up" when touched by another man. The degree of intimacy that develops within a committed group enables its members to confront negative assumptions about loving other men and to forge a new path toward emotional integration. Philip Culbertson speaks for many when he says:

> It will mean a new effort to form men-only prayer groups in which men learn to pray spontaneously, to touch each other tenderly and often, without fear, and to love other men in that group with a love like that between David and Jonathan, or between Jesus and the disciple whom he loved, men who pray together as they hold each other in their arms.[22]

The Value of Men's Groups

In *A Circle of Men: The Original Manual for Men's Support Groups*, Bill Kauth has identified fifteen topics of conversation which challenge common masculine assumptions and can lead men toward growth and empowerment.[23] Aaron Kipnis has catalogued twelve tasks of mature masculinity that men's groups would find beneficial to explore.[24] Likewise, Sam Keen has developed a series of exercises for men's groups to undertake which facilitate helpful reflection and conversation. A review of Keen's topical exercises illustrates the possibilities of a group's exploration:

• Recovering your personal manhood.
• Warfare, conquest and competition.
• Power and other values.
• Work, money and vocation.
• Sex, love and intimacy.
• Feelings and emotions.[25]

The following review summarizes three of the consistent themes which emerge when men assemble together to share their inner lives: *being a son, being a father*, and *being a lover*.

Being a Son

Chapter 4 named the "father wound" as the psychological consequence of an absent or abusive father. It has had a devastating impact upon contemporary men. In men's groups, strong masculine support is available as men uncover and express grief over the loss of their fathers. In other words, in groups men discover companions or "allies." According to Diamond,

> If we are to survive and prosper, we need the ongoing support of a few good men. You might think of these men as allies. I like the word ally. For me it suggests someone who is compassionate, friendly, and helpful. There is a gentleness and kindness implied. But ally also brings to mind the warrior energy of men who support each other under fire.[26]

The uncommon experience of relating to other men as friends and not as competitors occurs in groups such as these. As noted above, men are not used to masculine support for personal efforts of integration or healing. Yet, within the context of these groups, men discover others who will support them in their quest for wholeness. Richard Rohr and Joseph Martos call this experience of masculine support "male mothering."[27] Noting that "our woundedness as men can only be healed through an experience of union," Rohr/Martos recognize the value of men gathering together to support each other and impart "masculine energy."[28]

Ultimately, the goal of men's work is to allow a man to break free of the debilitating effects of the "father wound." Diamond notes:

> I can't forget the past and all the disappointments I experienced as a child. They are part of the fabric of my life. Yet I can stop blaming my father for what I never received. He loved me as well as he was able. Life is too short to allow past hurts to ruin the beauty of the present. My father is precious to me, and through him I am linked forever to all men back to the beginning of human history.[29]

This resonates with masculine spirituality's appreciation of the "non-renewable resource of the elder male."[30] As long as men are locked into emotional patterns of ambivalence or hostility toward their own father, they will be unable to appreciate the gift of elder males within the community. Robert Bly notes that many young men have been so wounded by their own fathers that they are unable to trust any authority figure. This results in men projecting their anger onto external masculine structures. He points to the increasing hatred of the father in television shows and movies. Bly posits that young scriptwriters, fueled by unresolved anger, ridicule their father by lampooning television fathers in evening situation comedies.[31] He suggests that when men are able to resolve their "father issues," then the insight and wisdom of previous generations becomes available to them.[32] Rohr and Martos call this mature masculine "grandfather energy" and demonstrate its value in the life of men.[33] Rohr explains it this way:

> We all need to be assured from time to time that we're doing the right thing. We are not sure where we stand because no one is there to reassure us. Sometimes we just need to hear from someone who believes in us, but who believes in us enough also to challenge us. Suddenly, the assurance and self-confidence are there, almost by magic, and almost embarrassingly so. It is humbling and wonderful to be a spiritual son.[34]

To summarize, men's groups become the place where a man can experience the challenge and support necessary to heal his "father wound." It is in the company of other men that healing masculine energy is transmitted, and a man's internal equilibrium can be restored and replenished.

Being a Father

Another value of men's gatherings is that they provide men the forum to examine their roles as fathers. There are several challenges that men face as fathers. First, it can be argued that men experience more parenting challenges than did fathers of previous generations. Escalating violence, runaway substance abuse and addictions, economic hardships and family dysfunction have increased at an alarming rate. Solutions to these problems are not forthcoming. As a result, today's fathers often find themselves ill-equipped to cope with a complex web of problems or to transmit paternal wisdom to their children. Second, men run the risk of unwittingly repeating the parenting mistakes of their fathers. Psychological theory informs us that we parent our children as we were parented. Without enlightenment, guidance, and support, men can perpetuate the damaging child rearing practices of the past. Third, Kipnis submits that in the past forty years, mothers have been the primary caregivers of children in the United States. This "exiling of, and ignoring the father"[35] has left men without solid masculine models from which to draw in their own attempt to be fathers to their children.

Men's gatherings provide educational opportunities for men in their parenting quest. Kipnis discovered that

...those of us with children are committed to being active, engaged parents. We're also healing our own childhood wounds by ensuring that our children don't grow up with the same loss we felt. Unlike our fathers, however, we now have a community of men that supports this ideal and acknowledges it as a masculine activity in every way.[36]

One of the ways that these groups encourage fathers to embrace their parenting role is to challenge them to explore their capacity for tenderness and nurturing—a foreign concept to many. Men's groups teach that "men don't seem to nurture in exactly the same manner as women, but that doesn't mean that what we offer is any less significant. It's separate, different, and equally important."[37]

There are two important tasks of masculinity that take place when men become actively involved as fathers. First, men provide the masculine energy to their children which was deficient in their own childhood. Having struggled with the consequences of their own "father wound," men are now able to be present to their children in such a way that they convey commitment, love and tenderness. Many men report great moments of healing in their lives as they nurture their children. Diamond suggests that active parenting has its rewards for fathers as well as children:

> It permits us to make contact with the lost boy within ourselves and thus connect with our own lost humanity. We no longer have to pretend to be men. We feel it from the inside, sometimes for the first time in our lives.[38]

Throughout this work, much of the discussion revolving around the "father wound" has been specifically related to its effect upon boys. It is important to recognize, however, that a girl suffers equally significant losses when her father is absent or abusive. Psychologists note that the father functions in a unique role for his daughter. He is the filter through which his daughter forms her ability to relate to men. In this capacity, he is more important than her mother. Kipnis recognizes as much:

> But it isn't only our sons whom we initiate into the outer world; we do this for our daughters as well....(W)e provide our daughters an opportunity to have a positive relationship with a man. I believe that most of the anti-male invective today comes from women who have had a negative relationship with their fathers. A girl's

positive relationship with a present and involved father builds the foundation for balanced relations with men in her adult life.[39]

Men's groups provide a forum for sharing ideas and information about effective parenting, and support men as they seek to interrupt abusive or unhealthy patterns of child rearing. They contribute to the education of the next generation of children that is rooted in mutuality, cooperation, commitment, passion, justice and equality.

Being a Lover

As has been noted in several places throughout this work, many men have conflicted ideas and feelings about their capacity to give and receive love. Arnold calls a man's capacity for love "the desire to give of himself to another person, and to share in life's experiences, joys, and struggles with another."[40] The conflict many men experience in their ability to love relates to an underdeveloped masculine psyche. In other words, "the healthier the man, the healthier his inner lover."[41] As men seek a greater measure of psychological integration, they will be able to experience a more profound sense of their loving capacities. Men's groups provide a supportive environment for men to grapple with issues of sexuality and relationship.

A vibrant men's group will not allow its members to remain fixated on the sexual aspect of loving. While these groups do share honestly about sexual matters, they introduce a much larger perspective of loving to its participants. Any discussion of man-as-lover that limits its focus to genital sexuality is too myopic. Men have a capacity for far deeper passion and love than is expressed in physical lovemaking,[42] and masculine gatherings explore all the possibilities of loving expression. Men's groups share sexual concerns and questions, but, more importantly, they empower a man to "remain connected to those around him— wife, lover, children, and friends."[43]

In these settings, men can reflect honestly upon their deepest concerns about loving relationships. One area of contemplation that is emerging in men's groups is the issue of male co-dependence, of men giving too much in relationships. Kipnis shares the focus of his group when he writes,

> One of the primary concerns we had as young men was our relationships with the other sex. This continues to be an arena of fascination, frustration and pain for us today. We are trying to improve our relationships with women, to have more balance and harmony while still keeping passion and pleasure alive. We want to avoid losing ourselves and our dreams in pursuit of women and to feel whole and independent of our relationships.[44]

Kipnis notes that male co-dependency often begins when a boy is trained to be "mother's little helper."[45] Within this dynamic, boys are taught that a woman's rewards of acceptance and nurture can be gained only by pleasing their mothers. This pattern of relationship is perpetuated for many as they enter the world of dating and marriage. Since men haven't been taught to value their own feelings, the only way they can experience deep feeling is at the hand of a woman. In other words, "only a woman can supply the missing essence."[46] Kipnis identifies this inequity:

> Most of us, however, had become accustomed to habitually being men who give too much. We often betrayed our own feelings, hopes, and desires because we thought we could not be loved just for who we are—only for what we do. We measured our worth by our capacity to caretake a woman.[47]

A challenge for men is to develop their own capacity for self-nurturance. The invitation and fortification of other men provides the perspective necessary to examine relational assumptions. As men cultivate the art of mindfulness, they can learn how to meet their own emotional needs and, thus, free themselves from the bondage to WOMAN. Sam Keen submits that "so long as we define ourselves to unconscious images of WOMAN we remain in exile from the true mystery and power of manhood."[48]

Another area of reflection is the obstacle that men experience when it comes to developing intimate relationships with other men. Sam Keen recognizes the need of men to develop intimate male friends when he writes,

> We need same sex friends because there are types of validation and acceptance that we receive only from our gendermates. There is much about our experience as men that can only be shared with, and understood by, other men. There are stories we can tell only to those who have wrestled with the same demons and been wounded by the same angels. Only men understand the secret fears that go with the territory of masculinity.[49]

As noted earlier, many contemporary men suffer from homophobic tendencies which limit their capacity for loving, non-sexual relationships with other men. This is borne out in sociological studies which indicate that men have few, if any, intimate friends of the same sex.[50] Many men are mistrustful of intimacy as they equate it with femininity. As a result, men are limited to buddies and pals, while true camaraderie or fellowship escapes them. Shallow masculine relationships have not been the norm throughout history. Anthropological research demonstrates that men have had the capacity for vibrant, vigorous intimate relationships with others for millennia. Robert Bly makes this cross-cultural observation:

> To judge by men's lives in New Guinea, Kenya, North Africa, the pygmy territories, Zulu lands, and in the Arab and Persian culture flavored by Sufi communities, men have lived together in heart unions and soul connections for hundreds of thousands of years.[51]

Philip Culbertson identifies four reasons that men are incapable of sustaining intimate relationships with other men. First, men have not been taught to value mutuality, cooperation and vulnerability—three essential characteristics of intimate relationships. Men may try to interact with their wives or girlfriends in this manner, because it is a "safe" expression of emotions. But to risk an intimate relationship with another man is beyond the acceptable range of possibilities for most contemporary men.[52] Second, he notes that there is an unspoken societal assumption that intimacy necessarily leads to sex.[53] This supposition falls into the trap illustrated above, that love and passion are limited to genital sexual expression. Given these assumptions, and the powerful bond that can occur during lovemaking, it can be understood why men shy away from intimacy.

Third, there are not many models of intimate, same-sex friendships for men prevalent in our culture. As a result, intimate friendships take on a falsely defined sexual character. Culbertson notes that "when men form close friendships with other men, it is symptomatic of our sexually sick society that so many people are quick to jump to conclusions."[54] Finally, he submits that homophobia restricts men's capacity for intimate relationships with other men. Culbertson points to a deep-seated fear within some men: the fear that by loving a man deeply, they themselves may actually be homosexual in orientation. He writes:

> It may help to understand that erotic feelings are a natural part of a deep same-sex friendship, and while they are normal, it is not necessary that they be acted upon genitally. The fear that American men have of such friendships is ultimately not a fear of others, but a fear of themselves—a fear that they will be overcome by their own unexpected homoerotic urge and "act the woman."[55]

Men's groups that engage in honest exploration and discussion of issues such as these do much to assist men in their emotional development as lovers. They can teach men that they don't need to be enslaved to women, or be afraid of loving men. First, they can encourage men to develop boundaries in their relationships with others, so that mutuality can be the hallmark of their loving. They can also prepare men to trust, and even enjoy intimate feelings toward other men. Gatherings such as these provide men with the opportunity to touch each other and, in doing so, discover that such acts don't lead to genital sexual expression. They can challenge men to examine prevalent cultural assumptions about what it means to be a loving man, and encourage them to integrate romantic passion, generosity, compassion and ecstatic joy into their emotional and spiritual life.

Initiation Rites

To this point, I have demonstrated the value of masculine spirituality for adult men. The authors represented in these pages have illustrated the ways that intentional men's gatherings heal men, inform them, and provide them with support to develop a mature masculine personality. The relationship of the men's movement to young men and boys has yet to be examined. While the men's movement offers great hope for men who are at mid-life or beyond, the question unanswered as of yet is, How does masculine spirituality inform the life of younger men? A review of the reflections of authors relative to initiation rites will attempt to answer this question.

The consensus of authors writing in the field of masculine psychology and spirituality is that a primary deficit in the common masculine experience is a lack of initiatory experiences for young men. Contemporary culture is "obsessed with manliness" but fails to provide a way for boys to enter into the mature masculine community.[56] Initiatory rites take a young man through a ritual process that introduces him to the community of men. Within a tribal context, initiatory rituals were designed to take boys from the world of women, and to place them in the world of men. Anthropological studies demonstrate the necessity of initiating boys into manhood. Diamond writes:

> In the first cross-cultural study of manhood, anthropologist David Gilmore found that becoming a man is a process that must be achieved through some sort of stressful series of tests that begin with boys being separated, sometimes forcefully, from the women of the tribe....In most cultures throughout the world, boys cannot become men except through a rite of passage.[57]

While the shape and construct of these initiatory rituals varied from culture to culture, the common denominator was that they were intended to "connect young men to the depth of the masculine soul, the spirit of nature, and the community as a whole."[58]

As was noted in Chapter 4, one of the primary challenges of the young man is to psychologically separate himself from the control of the feminine in his life.[59] Initiation rituals provide the capacity to accomplish that task. This is not to promote an anti-feminine bias in young men. Rather, as has been discussed in greater lengths in the last chapter, men need to establish a masculine identity that is balanced and integrated. Culbertson recognizes that women have been at this task for some time, and he echoes the call of many for men to begin such differentiation.[60] Keen recognizes the historical basis of initiation rituals and their ability to facilitate the necessary degree of separation:

> Premodern societies knew the overwhelming power of WOMAN and that boys could only emerge into manhood if they separated from her and entered for a time into an all-male world. Male rites of passage were designed to allow boys to escape from WOMAN'S world long enough to discover the shape of man's world.[61]

Initiation rites were not limited to helping boys separate from an inordinate feminine influence. They were a way for boys to enter into the world of vibrant adult masculinity. As such, women are not capable of leading boys into this arena. Try as they might, women don't have the capacity to "transmit masculine energy." Kipnis notes:

> Not a single one of us felt that our manhood had come from our mothers. They nurtured, comforted, educated and sang to us; they nurtured us when we were sick, taught us manners and protected us from various things, including the abuses of our fathers. But they couldn't teach us how to become men.[62]

The Absence of Initiation

Robert Bly calls the lack of masculine initiation "a wound in the chest" of young men.[63] This resonates with the writings of Moore and Gillette who suggest that initiation rituals are valuable insofar as they enable a boy to begin the necessary process of psychological discrimination and differentiation which leads to manhood. They note that "a man who cannot 'get it together' is a man who has probably not had the opportunity to undergo ritual initiation into the deep structures of manhood."[64] This resonates with Arnold's suggestion that the majority of men today are never "educated and nurtured into adult masculinity."[65]

The sociological implications that surround the lack of ritual initiation are profound. Several authors suggest that urban street gangs are a result of uninitiated young men attempting to initiate themselves into manhood. Bly notes that "when you look at a gang, you are looking...at young men who have no older men around them at all."[66] Richard Rohr points to the following as evidence that there are no authentic experiences of initiation for young men today:

- gang violence.
- gender identity confusion.
- romanticization of war.
- aimless violence.
- homophobia.[67]

Moore and Gillette place the phenomena of street gangs within the larger context of pseudo-initiatory rituals that take place in the west today. They decry the lack of authentic initiatory rituals:

Our own culture has pseudo-rituals instead. There are many pseudo-initiations for men in our culture. Conscription into the military is one. The fantasy is that the humiliation and forced nonidentity of boot camp will "make a man out of you." The gangs of our major cities are another manifestation of pseudo-initiation and so are the prison systems, which, in large measure, are run by gangs.[68]

The presence of such pseudo-rituals testifies to the lack of authentic masculine initiation. Moore and Gillette categorize these incidents as pseudo-events for two reasons. First, they initiate boys into a masculinity that is "skewed, stunted, and false." The masculine persona that gangs and military training idealize is often very adolescent in its nature, and it leads to an ethic of abuse. Second, most of these initiations are not concerned at all with ritual process. As such, they posit that these initiations are short-sighted, and miss necessary existential and transcendent dimensions of masculine experience. This leads to egocentric manifestations of individuality, competition, power and control.[69]

Elements of Ritual Initiation

Cross-cultural research suggests that there are common themes or motifs of masculine initiation. Patrick Arnold summarizes this research in his book, *Wildmen, Warriors and Kings*. In this work, he notes that there are three stages to the initiatory process.

Departure. The first stage in any process of ritual masculine initiation was an enforced departure from the world of women. This step communicated in "vivid and decisive" tones that 1) the young boy could no longer remain a child, and 2) he could no longer remain in the domain of women. In many cultures the men of the village or tribe came to the boy's home at a pre-arranged time, and abducted him from the care and control of his mother. In other words, he had to become a man. Reflecting upon the current crisis of masculinity, Arnold notes that "it now takes men years of struggle with guilt and self-confidence, alone and in psychotherapy, to negotiate a stage that once occurred in a few days or weeks."[70]

Ordeal of Initiation. The next stage of initiation occurred in a sacred place where only men were allowed to enter. Arnold submits that men "need holy space at a distance from the feminine world." In these sacred places, rituals took place over a number of days which were designed to sever a man's dependence upon women and link his personal manhood to the welfare of the whole tribe. During this stage of initiation, men forced the boys to undergo "painful but carefully controlled trials that inevitably involved humiliation and mutilation." While the contemporary shudders at such "abusive behavior," Arnold suggests that there were focused and beneficial consequences to these acts. To the tribal mind, ritual humiliation was necessary to disdain the world of "boys and women." In other words, the boy had to make a break with his childlike and feminine self. Ritual mutilation was designed to teach the boy that "becoming a man is a painful, wounding, but proud experience." During this period of initiation, the boys were told the great stories of the tribes and their ancestors. They were told that they were expected to live lives of "ordinary greatness," not for themselves, but for the well-being of their community. At the end of the initiatory ritual, when the elders were convinced that the boys' emotional link to the world of woman was shattered, they "officially and ritually accepted them as men." They were no longer children, but adult members of the community.[71]

Return and Reintegration. In the final stage of initiation, the men returned to the village amidst great celebration and festivities. The young men, clothed in their ritual garments and/or adult names, appeared to the village for the first time, reborn as new men. The community recognized the transformation that had taken place in the life of the boys, and that they were now part of the circle of men. From this point forward, they were expected to function as adult members of the tribe and participate with "lives of concrete and everyday heroism."[72]

There are a number of implications that a study of initiatory rituals pose for masculine spirituality. Richard Rohr suggests that there are no initiation rituals that provide young men with the experience of separation-initiation-return noted above. "Boy Scouts, Confirmation classes, Lions and Elks clubs have tried to substitute, but with little spiritual effect."[73] Commenting upon the lack of authentic initiatory rituals, Arnold observes:

The most important service the church could perform in this regard is to take seriously once again its ancient role of ritually

initiating young males into responsible adulthood....(T)he church
can make positive, though limited, contributions toward marking
the initiation of boys into manhood, beginning at the local parish
and diocesan levels.[74]

He portrays what such organized efforts might look like.
First, adult men would take younger men into some sort of
wilderness setting for an initiation weekend. A sacred ritual
would inaugurate the weekend experience. In this ritual, boys
would participate in some symbolic activity which signified the
death of the *puer* existence. Arnold notes that this could include
some sort of significant haircut or tattoo, something that leaves
behind a palpable mark that ritualizes the transition from boy-
hood to manhood. Next, the rite would continue with an
accounting of what is expected of the boys as they enter the
world of men. In this setting, the older men could share their
personal accounts of masculinity and offer their wisdom and
vision to the initiates. At the conclusion of the initiatory rituals,
some sort of baptism could be celebrated during which the boys
would receive a new name, one that identifies their birthing into
the world of men.[75]

Arnold stresses the importance of making these weekend
experiences ones where boys are physically, emotionally and
spiritually challenged. Liturgical reform has clearly demonstrated that ceremony for its own sake is generally quite ineffective.
These gatherings of young men require creative deliberation on
the part of those who plan the events to ensure that the boys
know that they are experiencing an initiation into a new way of
life. Arnold points to the success of endeavors such as an
"Outward Bound" weekend that combine wilderness survival
skills, team building experiences and group reflection as examples of effective challenge.

At the end of the weekend, a return might incorporate a wel-
coming ceremony where the boys experience a ritual acceptance
into the adult life of the parish. He writes:

After these rituals, the church as well as the family ought then to treat the youths in a new and adult fashion; the young men could take a more visible part in church decisions and ceremonies, and enjoy new rights and duties at home. The handing over of the car keys to the boy, for example, would be a very meaningful expression of this trust to everyone.[76]

The Mature Masculine Vision

Perhaps one of the most significant offerings that elder men can make to the next generation is the developing vision of an authentic, mature, passionate, community-based masculinity. Boys need to hear from the mouths of older men that "masculine spirituality contributes distinctive and irreplaceable graces to the human culture, such as fighting for what you believe in, loving freedom, and taking responsibility for others."[77] The next generation of men must know that "there is no end to the ways that we can express a spirited and careful sense of manhood,"[78] that "the challenge of the masculine spirit is to rebuild society through concerted social activism."[79] Dwight Judy prays:

Send me into the village square, send me into the schools, send me into the day camps for children, send me into the task of creating beauty, send me into the business world to create more jobs, send me into the political world to struggle for the values I hold dear, send me into the earth as her son, to love her and to cherish her. Send me to help create the "thousand healths and hidden isles" not even yet imagined.[80]

It is essential that the next generation of men know that shame-based masculinity is destructive at its core, that there is cause for pride in their gender, and that, as Richard Rohr notes, "The spiritual man in mythology, in literature, and in the great world religions has an excess of life, he knows he has it, makes no apology for it and finally recognizes that he does not need to protect it. It is for others."[81] Those men who follow this generation can learn to live hopefully, love passionately and serve with

commitment and zeal. Patrick Arnold calls for men to engage in
a life that is committed to the "God-path," that is, one who passionately loves God and serves others.[82]

As has been noted throughout this work, the image of the
Warrior holds profound power for masculine psychology and
spirituality. To summarize the authentic masculine visions, Bill
Kauth notes:

> We believe the word "Warrior" best describes the spirit of the
> masculine psyche. The New Warrior knows who he is, what he
> wants and where he is going. Simply put, he is a man without
> guilt, shame, or apology. He has integrity. He holds himself
> accountable for his own actions. He is wild and gentle, tough and
> loving, fierce and perceptive. He comes from a tribe of men. He
> is not a savage. He is a Warrior of the Heart.[83]

Summary

In this chapter, I have reviewed those authors who value discovering masculinity through the experience of a community.
First, I conducted a brief analysis of the need for intentional gatherings of men that are rooted in developing community, intimacy
and cooperation. Next, I reviewed the considerations of those
authors who have chronicled the benefits of men gathering
together to reflect, challenge and care for each other. Third, I
reviewed the basic discussion about the lack of authentic masculine initiation rites in our culture. Finally, I presented the considerations of authors in this work who have painted a picture of a
mature masculine presence for the future. The authors represented in this work universally agree that the time is ripe for a new
breed of man who is prayerful, loving, just, and committed to
emerge upon the contemporary consciousness of our time.

Epilogue

Oliver Wendell Holmes once said that a mind stretched beyond its boundaries never returns to its original condition. In writing this book, my hope has been that I could stretch the readers' minds beyond any pre-conceptions to see masculinity and men in a new way. Men are not the beasts that some make them out to be, nor are they the only source of blessing to the world. Rather, men are bearers of a great and proud tradition that has much to offer the world. In light of this, I began my review of masculine spirituality with two questions in mind. The first was, "Can there be an authentic masculine spirituality or God-path that is dedicated to men and yet not be anti-woman?" The second was, "What do men have to offer subsequent generations?" This work has pointed to answers for both of these questions.

Men, both inside organized religion and in non-religious settings, are engaged in a quest for the masculine spirit. Depth psychology, anthropology, sociology, scriptural scholarship, and theological reflection all indicate that developing masculine spirituality is not only possible, but an essential task for our time. Despite some of the misandrist notions that abound in both church and society, it is important to recognize that being a man is good, it is a gift. Men think, act, pray and love in ways that are unique to them, and, as such, masculine spirituality seeks to unfold men's discovery of God. Any past abuse of women, children, minorities or the environment by our forefathers doesn't negate the enormous benefit that men bring to the world today. So it becomes imperative that men seek to experience a mature masculine spirituality, that of the "new warrior." The God-path that masculine spirituality charts is clear. To be a "new warrior," men must engage in a gritty, passionate, fearful, loving encounter with God which leads them to a new quality and depth of life. Like Israel, men who embark on this quest toward God will bear the marks of their struggle. But this stretching and strengthening will bear rich fruit. As men develop their authentic masculine spirit, they will appreciate the rich reservoirs of strength within. Having moved toward integration of their own feminine traits and characteristics, these "new warriors" will esteem women and honor their pilgrimage toward God.

As to the second question, mature masculinity offers a myriad of gifts for the next generation. First, men can expand the horizons of love, commitment, passion, leadership, and justice for their children. Mature men can offer society images of mutuality, cooperation, and harmony with others and the planet. They can teach their sons that passion, commitment, focus, spirituality, and justice are hallmarks of the masculine spirit which spring from the deep reservoirs of a man's soul. Next, men can extend a spirit of loving protection, encouragement, independence and equality to their daughters. The "new warrior" recognizes that women are co-heirs in God's economy of creation, and offers them respect and gratitude for the gifts and presence they bring to the world. Finally, men can confirm that masculine power is good and not something to be feared. The power of the "new warrior" will advance the restoration of a society that languishes in ambivalence, hostility, and despair. The contribution of men possessed of a vibrant and committed spirit has been envisioned, but not yet fully realized. But, with the "world waiting in the wings," the time for rebuilding is overdue.

It has been said that our generation thirsts for authentic spiritual experiences. All too often, practices of spirituality reside at extreme poles of either piety disconnected from the struggle for justice, or social action severed from authentic encounters with the divine. The challenge for masculine spirituality is to provide men an embodied path that leads them to the vibrant, passionate, gentle, liberating God being discovered anew by men and women around the world.

Notes

Chapter 1

1. See Tom Burkett, "Are Men Obsolete?" *XO Magazine* 1 (July 1994): 10–12. In this article, a popular critique on the assault of "politically correct masculinity" is addressed.

2. Mary Daly, *Beyond God the Father* (Boston: Beacon, 1973), p. 75.

3. See Neal King and Martha McCaughey, "Rape Is All Too Thinkable for Quite the Normal Sort of Man," *Los Angeles Times*, February 17, 1990.

4. Patrick Arnold offers a critique of the radical feminist challenge to the validity of masculine influences in history, and in doing so notes some thirty-two fields of beneficent endeavor to which men have contributed. See his *Wildmen, Warriors and Kings* (New York: Crossroad, 1992), p. 59.

5. Philip Culbertson, *The New Adam: The Future of Male Spirituality* (Minneapolis: Fortress Press, 1992), p. 3.

6. *Ibid.*, p. 6. Additionally, Patrick Arnold sees the imperative for masculine separation to be based on a growing intellectual and cultural inability to recognize positive masculinity. As such, there is a growing desire in the men's movement to conduct masculine reflection in a context that affirms men's insights and contributions. Arnold, *Wildmen, Warriors and Kings*, p. 42.

7. See Arnold Van Gennep's *The Rites of Passage*, translated by M. Vizedom (Chicago: University of Chicago Press, 1960).

8. In his work, *Thresholds of Initiation* (Middletown: Wesleyan University Press, 1967), Joseph L. Henderson offers an in-depth study of the values of initiation rites and their relationship to psychological theory.

9. A consistent theme in the literature of the men's movement is that women's studies have forged a path for an authentic vision of personal liberation. Culbertson notes that for some time now, women have understood their societal oppression more clearly than men, and as a result have taken significant steps to reconstruct a path for recovery and integration that men can follow. Culbertson, *The New Adam*, p. 6.

10. It should be noted that while men's studies is a relatively new field, there is nevertheless a great deal to be written about the various concepts of "manliness." Issues such as gender discrimination against men, legal challenges to accepted norms of mother-preferential parenting, masculine addictions, and sociological implications of sexual orientation are emerging in both popular and academic literature. This work will address the broader based issues only insofar as they touch the topic of masculine spirituality. It could be argued that everything that concerns a man is part and parcel of his spiritual life. While that is true, this work will be specifically focused on the emerging tradition of masculine spirituality and its constitutive components.

11. Kipnis suggests that a man who suffers from psychic numbness is likely to find ways to feel through such addictions as excitement and sex. Aaron R. Kipnis, *Knights Without Armor: A Practical Guide for Men in Quest of Masculine Soul* (New York: Tarcher/Pedigree, 1991), p. 17.

12. In his work with men's therapy groups, Samuel Osherson confronts the prevailing loneliness that men feel. He speaks of the inability of a man to share with others, especially other men, his loneliness, shame and despair. *Wrestling with Love* (New York: Fawcett-Columbine, 1992), pp. 49–52.

13. "A useful definition of spirituality, then, is as follows: the human desire or urge to establish a relationship with that Power or Being that

transcends our human limitations, including our gender-specific limitations, without invalidating or destroying those limitations." Culbertson,
The New Adam, p. 109.

14. Medical research indicates that a lack of tactile stimulation in the first
sixteen months may actually result in a deficiency in the growth of nerve
endings. It has been demonstrated that tactile stimulation is an important
factor in stimulating the growth of nerve tissues and their protective coat-
ings. Kipnis suggests that since neural pathways are still being formed
during this period of time, a deficit in tactile stimulation may inhibit neural development, and the difference in verbal dexterity between boys and
girls may be related to such deficit. Kipnis, *Knights Without Armor*, p. 24.

15. *Ibid.*

16. There are characteristically two results of the estrangement between
a son and his mother. To summarize: the boy makes the psychological
connection between his personal mother and all women, and then is
either a) obsessed with women, looking for them to meet his every
security and affective emotional need, or b) lives out of a state of anxiety and fear about women, and looks for every opportunity to degrade
and injure the feminine, both in himself and actual women.

17. See Sam Keen's *Fire in the Belly* (New York: Bantam Books, 1991)
for an assessment of the dependency relationship between men and
"WOMAN."

18. See Gerald Coleman, "Today's Seminarians and the Role of the
Priest," *America*, 164 (April 27, 1991): 466–468.

19. As Richard Rohr suggests, "To believe in father-love is for most of
us the greater leap of faith. Many who want to throw out the wonderful
and sexually charged word 'Father' (for God) are the last ones who
should do it." Richard Rohr & Joseph Martos, *The Wildman's Journey:
Reflections on Male Spirituality* (Cincinnati: St. Anthony Messenger
Press, 1992), p. 94.

20. Arnold suggests that men nurture in a different way than women do,
and that since there is such a deficit of authentic masculine strength in

this culture, men don't know what masculine nurturing looks like. Consequently anything that appears soft in God is dismissed outright as feminine. Patrick J. Arnold, *Wildmen, Warriors and Kings*, p. 47.

21. Kipnis suggests that the mother finds the boy's infantile sexuality disturbing, and communicates the message that the penis is a "bad thing." *Knights Without Armor*, p. 44.

22. Arnold, *Wildmen, Warriors and Kings*, p. 94.

23. In his work *Absent Fathers/Lost Sons* (Boston: Shambalah Press, 1991) Guy Corneau develops this theme by listing statistics that indicated that one in five children lives in a fatherless home.

24. Corneau writes, "This lack of attention from the father results in the son's inability to identify with his father as a means of establishing his own masculine identity. Similarly, a son deprived of the confirmation and security that might have been provided by his father's presence is unable to advance to adulthood." *Ibid.*, p. 13.

25. *Ibid.*, pp. 19–20.

26. The authors suggest that James A. Doyle's *The Masculine Experience* (New York: W.C. Brown, 1983) provides an in-depth evaluation of this masculine persona.

27. Rohr/Martos use the archetypical image of the "Holy Man" or the "Wild Man" to characterize the completed stage of a man's individuation. *The Wildman's Journey*, p. 25.

28. Culbertson, *The New Adam.*, pp. 110–111.

29. *Ibid.*, p. 110.

30. *Ibid.*, p. 111.

31. *Ibid.*, p. 158.

32. Arnold, *Wildmen, Warriors and Kings*, p. 51.

33. *Ibid.*, p. 29.

34. *Ibid.*, p. 47.

35. *Ibid.*, p. 65.

Chapter 2

1. Brian Wren, *What Language Shall I Borrow? God-Talk in Worship: A Male Response to Feminist Theology* (New York: Crossroad Books, 1989), p. 64.

2. "Language is not merely an external feature of reality, but, as the major traditions of social theory have asserted in recent decades, language is the main bearer and transmitter of the social structure." Karen Bloomquist, "Let God Be God: The Theological Necessity of Depatriarchializing God," in *Our Naming of God: Problems and Prospects of God-Talk Today*, edited by Carl E. Braaten (Minneapolis: Fortress Press, 1989), p. 47.

3. Ruth C. Duck, *Gender and the Name of God: The Trinitarian Baptismal Formula* (New York: Pilgrim Press, 1991), p. 3.

4. "The biblical experience of God is not in concepts that are argued and reasoned about (though people do think and reason in its pages), but of the Holy One who encounters us and whose reality impinges on us." Wren, *What Language Shall I Borrow?* p. 105.

5. "Liturgical language may be revelatory; that is, through it we may enter into deeper understanding of and communion with God." Duck, *Gender and the Name of God*, p. 20.

6. "In both the Hebrew and Christian Scriptures, a way of life is presented to God's people to follow. That way of life is inseparable from the history that has revealed their God. Using Scripture in Christian ethics, therefore, must be rooted in that history and the One it reveals." William C. Spohn, *What Are They Saying About Scripture and Ethics?* (New York: Paulist Press, 1983), p. 1.

7. Donald G. Bloesch, *Battle for the Trinity: The Debate Over Inclusive God-Language* (Ann Arbor: Servant Publications, 1985).

8. G.B. Caird, *The Language and Imagery of the Bible* (London: Duckworth, 1980), pp. 18–19.

9. Bloesch, *Battle for the Trinity*, p. 13.

10. In the field of psychological development alone, the understanding of the tendency of the human being to "project" personal desires and needs onto a God image has provided crucial insight into the nature of God imaging. In the words of one psychiatrist, "We make gods out of our parents and parents out of our gods."

11. Bloomquist, *Let God be God*, p. 53.

12. Sallie McFague, *Models of God: Theology for an Ecological Nuclear Age* (Philadelphia: Fortress Press, 1989), p. 78.

13. From *Language About God—Opening the Door, by the Task Force on Language About God*, Advisory Council on Discipleship and Worship. From Minutes of the General Assembly of the United Presbyterian Church in the U.S.A., Part 1, 1975.

14. Kenneth Leech, *Soul Friend: The Practice of Christian Spirituality* (San Francisco: Harper & Row, 1977), p. 156.

15. Philip Culbertson, *The New Adam: The Future of Male Spirituality* (Minneapolis: Fortress Press, 1992), p. 112.

16. Matthew Linn, Sheila Fabricant Linn, and Dennis Linn, *Good Goats: Healing Our Image of God* (New York: Paulist Press, 1993), p. 42.

17. "The language of Christian scripture, tradition, theology, and worship developed within the social and political context of patriarchy, which marginalized and silenced women." Duck, *Gender and the Name of God*, p. 86.

18. "Gender issues are issues of justice. Male dominance permeates the fundamental intellectual quests of our civilization. It manifests itself in models of the economy, the recurring cult of toughness in politics, male violence toward women and children, and some aspects of the nuclear arms race." Wren, *What Language Shall I Borrow?* p. 6.

19. "Frequent use of masculine language for God in Christian worship, when feminine images are never used, is of concern to feminists because it both expresses and undergirds the sociopolitical system of patriarchy." Duck, *Gender and the Name of God*, p. 4.

20. "If God in his heaven is a father ruling his people, then it is in the nature of things and according to the divine plan and the order of the universe that society be male-dominated." Mary Daly, *Beyond God the Father* (Boston: Beacon Press, 1973), p. 13.

21. "The monarchical model is dangerous in our time: it encourages a sense of distance from the world; it attends only to the human dimension of the world; and it supports attitudes of either domination of the world or passivity towards it." McFague, *Models of God*, p. 69.

22. "Biblical faith forbids tangible graven images, but revels in a variety of intangible linguistic ones." Wren, *What Language Shall I Borrow?* p. 131.

23. *Ibid.*, p. 132.

24. "We are not naming ourselves, one another and our earth in ways commensurate with our own times but are using names from a bygone time. However helpful and healing these names may have been once upon a time, they are hurtful now. And Christian theology that is done on the basis of anachronistic naming is also hurtful." McFague, *Models of God*, p. 3.

25. Patrick J. Arnold, *Wildmen, Warriors and Kings: Masculine Spirituality and the Bible* (New York: Crossroad, 1992), p. 203.

26. *Ibid.*, pp. 203–204.

27. *Ibid.*

28. William Oddie, *What Will Happen To God? Feminism and the Reconstruction of Christian Belief* (San Francisco: Ignatius Press, 1988), p. 113.

29. *Ibid.*, p. 112.

30. *Ibid.*, p. 113.

31. "Now, it is clearly implied that in a humanitarian religion, based on solidarity and not on authority, no way of imagining God has priority over any other. God is in everything equally; furthermore, since we are autonomous beings, our own idea of God is right for us." *Ibid.*, p. 110.

32. *Ibid.*, p. 117.

33. "And the definitive symbol Father for God, which belongs if anything at all does to the domain of revelation rather than that of theological reflection or humanly constructed analogy, can have no meaning unless that meaning is perceived in the context of the relationship it implies." *Ibid.*, p. 93.

34. *Ibid.*, p. 123.

35. For a discussion on the evolution of patriarchy, see Gerder Lerner, *The Creation of Patriarchy* (New York: Oxford University Press, 1986), p. 243. A particular point that Lerner makes is that women were necessary and willing accomplices in the development of patriarchy.

36. Arnold, *Wildmen, Warriors and Kings*, p. 37.

37. "Patriarchy can more generally be defined as a male-dominant power structure in society in which all relationships are understood in terms of superiority or inferiority, and social cohesion is assured by the exercise of dominative power." Bloomquist, *Let God Be God*, p. 47.

38. Wren, *What Language Shall I Borrow?* p. 21.

39. Robert Moore and Douglas Gillette, *King, Warrior, Magician, Lover: Rediscovering the Archetypes of the Mature Masculine* (New York: HarperCollins, 1990), p. 17.

40. Arnold, *Wildmen, Warriors and Kings*, p. 37.

41. For an academic and yet manageable discussion on this issue, see

John Nicholson, *Men and Women: How Different Are They?* (Oxford: Oxford University Press, 1984).

42. "Some of the virtues that I would place in this category are self-possession, leadership, truthfulness, decisiveness, responsibility, closure, intelligence, inner authority, challenge, courage and risk taking." Rohr/Martos, *The Wildman's Journey*, p. 132.

43. For a review of the differences between the way that men and women think, see (Sharon Begley) "Gray Matters," and (Geoffrey Cowley), "Rethinking Nature and Nurture," in *Newsweek Magazine* (March 27, 1995): pp. 48–54.

44. Duck, *Gender and the Name of God*, p. 4.

45. "Trinity creates humankind as male and female. We are created in that otherness and togetherness so that this fundamental relationship can mirror the divine life. There are many ways in which we know human beings as Other: each person is Other, however like us they may be. There are also many webs of relationship where, through teamwork, cooperation, and organizing things together, human beings can glimpse, for a moment, the elusive marvel of the Trinity dance of love-in-relationship and, perhaps, weave new patterns on the divine loom or paint new pictures on the canvass of history." Wren, *What Language Shall I Borrow?* p. 53.

46. Moore and Gillette, *King, Warrior, Magician, Lover*, p. 17.

47. Wren, *What Language Shall I Borrow?* pp. 56–59.

48. In commenting on the topic of power, Culbertson notes that men have four kinds of power: "(1) the power to name; (2) the power to mobilize destructive aggression; (3) the power to organize societal, economic and political life; and (4) the power to direct others' uses of skills." Culbertson, *The New Adam*, p. 14.

49. *Ibid.*, p. 6.

50. Arnold, *Wildmen, Warriors and Kings*, p. 204.

51. See *ibid.*, pp. 203–204, for a list of masculine images that represent God in the scriptural texts.

52. "Rather than liquidate masculine theological metaphors, we ought to listen to what they are trying to say about God; rather than censor them from the church's life and worship, we might probe them for their wisdom." *Ibid.*, p. 203.

53. Culbertson, *The New Adam*, p. 115.

54. Culbertson identifies "texts of terror" within the biblical tradition which are threatening to contemporary views of masculine development. *Ibid.*, pp. 72–74.

55. Wren, *What Language Shall I Borrow?* p. 132.

56. Richard Rohr and Joseph Martos, *The Wildman's Journey*, p. 35.

57. "The masculine spiritual language of the biblical archetypes vastly enriches our imagination of God, our worship, and our theology. That our God-talk is unfortunately deficient in the feminine is no fair reflection on the aptness of masculine metaphors, and certainly no justification for their elimination from prayer and worship." Arnold, *Wildmen, Warriors and Kings*, p. 215.

Chapter 3

1. Sam Keen, *Fire in the Belly: On Being a Man* (New York: Bantam Books, 1991), p. 128.

2. Robert Moore and Douglas Gillette, *King, Warrior, Magician, Lover: Rediscovering the Archetypes of the Mature Masculine* (New York: HarperCollins Publishers, 1990), p. 9.

3. Bill Moyers, video *A Gathering of Men with Robert Bly* (New York: Public Television Corporation, 1990).

4. John Bradshaw, *Creating Love: The Next Great Stage of Growth* (New York: Bantam Books, 1992), p. 119.

5. Thomas Moore, *Care of the Soul: A Guide for Cultivating Depth and Sacredness in Everyday Life* (New York: HarperCollins Publishers, 1990), p. 5.

6. *Ibid.*, p. i.

7. Bradshaw, *Creating Love*, p. 116.

8. Moore, *Care of the Soul*, p. 5.

9. James Hillman, *Re-Visioning Psychology* (New York: HarperCollins Publishers, 1977).

10. Moore, *Care of the Soul*, p. 177.

11. Daniel C. Noel, "Soulful Spirituality: Reimagining a Spiritual Psychology," *The Quest* (Denville: Winter Edition, 1994), p. 41.

12. Richard Rohr, *Quest for the Grail* (New York: Crossroad, 1994), p. 48.

13. *Ibid.*

14. Bradshaw, *Creating Love*, p. 126.

15. *Ibid.*, p. 130.

16. Moore, *Care of the Soul*, p. xviii.

17. *Ibid.*, p. xiii.

18. Rohr, *Quest for the Grail*, p. 48.

19. For a concise examination of the relationship between body, soul and spirit in medicine, see Bernie Seigel, *Peace, Love and Healing: Bodymind Communication and the Path to Self-healing, an Exploration* (New York: Harper & Row, 1990). In this work, Seigel outlines the discovery and development of psychoneuroimmunology, that is "MindBody" medicine.

20. "Historically, soul is to be found in the spleen, the liver, the stom-

ach, the gall bladder, the intestines, the pituitary, and the lungs....Hillman and Sardello suggest this is the function of the body: to give us emotions and images proper to its highly articulated organs." Moore, *Care of the Soul*, p. 158.

21. *Ibid.*, p. 5.

22. *Ibid.*, p. 42.

23. "If we are not open to the unconscious, we are not open to the totality, and therefore usually not very open to God. Ego consciousness is just open to what *I* know (which is usually what I want to know). That means putting the lid on the unconscious, because the unconscious will be passionate, sexual, fiery, scary, wonderful, angry—all the things I don't want to feel because I might stop going to church." Rohr, *Quest for the Grail*, p. 48.

24. Moore/Gillette, *King, Warrior, Magician, Lover*, p. xvii.

25. Seigel, *Peace, Love and Healing*, p. 116.

26. Moore/Gillette, *The King Within: Accessing the King in the Male Psyche* (New York: Harper and Row, 1989), p. 9.

27. Patrick M. Arnold, *Wildmen, Warriors and Kings: Masculine Spirituality and the Bible* (New York: Crossroad, 1992), p. 27.

28. *Ibid.*, p. 26.

29. *Ibid.*

30. Jean Shinoda Bolen, *Gods in Everyman* (New York: Harper & Row, 1989), p. 6.

31. Moore/Gillette, *The King Within*, p. 33.

32. See Moore and Gillette, "The Archetype and Brain Structure" in Chapter One, and "Archetypes and the Limbic System" in Appendix B of *The King Within*. They suggest that archetypes originate in the reptilian brain, and pass upward through the paleomammalian and neomammalian brains, into the right brain, the seat of images and symbols. See p. 51.

33. See *ibid.*, pp. 33–35, for a concise review of the development of the collective unconscious from Freud to Jung.

34. Arnold, *Wildmen, Warriors and Kings*, p. 26.

35. Bolen, *Gods in Everyman*, p. 7.

36. Aaron R. Kipnis, *Knights Without Armor: A Practical Guide for Men in Quest of Masculine Soul* (New York: Tarcher, 1992), p. 106.

37. Arnold, *Wildmen, Warriors and Kings*, p. 85.

38. Moore/Gillette, *The King Within*, p. 9.

39. *Ibid.*, p. 102.

40. *Ibid.*, p. 30.

41. *Ibid.*, p. 61.

42. For a discussion of the bi-polar shadow of archetypal structure, see Moore/Gillette, *The King Within*, pp. 36–39.

43. *Ibid.*, p. 35.

44. See "Dancing the Four Quarters" in Moore/Gillette, *King, Warrior, Magician, Lover*, pp. 237–240, for an illustration of the inter-relationship between the archetypes in a man's psyche.

45. Moore/Gillette, *King, Warrior, Magician, Lover*, p. 44.

46. *Ibid.*, p. 49

47. *Ibid.*

48. *Ibid.*, p. 44.

49. *Ibid.*, p. 62.

50. *Ibid.*, p. 56.

51. *Ibid.*, pp. 51–52.

52. *Ibid.*, p. 62.

53. *Ibid.*, p. 178.

54. Rohr/Martos, *The Wildman's Journey: Reflections on Masculine Spirituality* (Cincinnati: St. Anthony Messenger Press, 1992), p. 199.

55. Moore/Gillette, *King, Warrior, Magician, Lover*, p. 75.

56. *Ibid.*, pp. 76–79.

57. *Ibid.*, p. 79.

58. Richard Rohr identifies the Shadow Warrior as the Black Knight/Dark Warrior. "Quite simply, the dark warrior is either not in submission to a king, or he is in submission to a bad king." *The Wildman's Journey*, p. 203.

59. For a discussion of the various manifestations of the Shadow Warrior, see Moore/Gillette, *King, Warrior, Magician, Lover*, pp. 90–94.

60. *Ibid.*, p. 79.

61. Rohr/Martos, *The Wildman's Journey*, p. 95.

62. *Ibid.*, p. 204.

63. Moore/Gillette, *King, Warrior, Magician, Lover*, pp. 102–106.

64. *Ibid.*, p. 107.

65. *Ibid.*, p. 100.

66. *Ibid.*, p. 110.

67. *Ibid.*, p. 118.

68. *Ibid.*, p. 120.

69. *Ibid.*, p. 121.

70. Rohr/Martos, *The Wildman's Journey*, p. 205.

71. See Philip Culbertson, *The New Adam: The Future of Male Spirituality*, for a discussion of shaming a boy's sexuality. Addressing the double bind messages that boys receive about sexuality, Culbertson notes, "Sex is dirty...and so you save it for someone you love." See p. 125.

72. Moore/Gillette, *King, Warrior, Magician, Lover*, pp. 131–139.

73. *Ibid.*, p. 141.

74. *Ibid.*, p. 36.

75. *Ibid.*, p. 43.

76. Rohr/Martos, *The Wildman's Journey*, p. 199.

77. Joseph Campbell with Bill Moyers, *The Power of Myth* (New York: Doubleday, 1988), p. 5.

78. "Because we lost the great mythic universe, we find ourselves in a post-Christian era dominated by rationalism, with its desire to understand and control. So we lack a mythic language that is nature-based or mystery-filled. Mythic language always points outward and upward, explaining how we are situated in a bigger picture or story." Rohr, *The Quest for the Grail*, p. 23.

79. "The late scholar and author Joseph Campbell did us a great service through his research into mythology. He was born Catholic, which he said gave him a great head start, but equally significant was the fact that he later became disillusioned with Catholicism because, he said, the Catholic Church lost the imaginal world." *Ibid.*, p. 21.

80. Joseph Campbell, *The Flight of the Wild Gander: Explorations in the Mythological Dimension* (New York: Viking Press, 1969), p. 73.

81. Rohr, *The Quest for the Grail*, p. 54.

82. Arnold, *Wildmen, Warriors and Kings*, p. 95.

83. *Ibid.*, p. 42.

84. Richard A. Underwood, "Living by Myth: Joseph Campbell, C.G. Jung, and the Religious Life Journey," *Paths to the Power of Myth: Joseph Campbell and the Study of Religion* (New York: Crossroad, 1990), pp. 27–28.

85. See Dwight H. Judy, *Healing the Male Soul: Christianity and the Mythic Journey* (New York: Crossroad Press, 1992), for a helpful demonstration of the "heroic" journey of masculine maturity.

86. Rohr, *Quest for the Grail*, p. 57.

87. Robert Bly, *Iron John: A Book About Men* (New York: Random House, 1992).

88. Moyers, *A Gathering of Men with Robert Bly*, PBS video.

89. Culbertson, *The New Adam*, p. 159.

Chapter 4

1. Sam Keen, *Fire in the Belly: On Being a Man* (San Francisco: Bantam Books, 1991), p. 35.

2. Alice Miller, *For Your Own Good: Hidden Cruelty in Child-Rearing and the Roots of Violence* (New York: Farrar, Straus, Giroux, 1983), notes that most commonly accepted methods of raising children in general, and boys in particular, are abusive at their core.

3. Keen, *Fire in the Belly*, pp. 35–36.

4. Dwight H. Judy, *Healing the Male Soul: Christianity and the Mythic Journey* (New York: Crossroad Publishing Company, 1992), p. 119.

5. Aaron Kipnis, *Knights Without Armor: A Practical Guide for Men in Quest of Masculine Soul* (New York: Tarcher/Pedigree Press, 1991), p. 37.

6. Jed Diamond, *The Warrior's Journey Home: Healing Men, Healing the Planet* (Oakland: New Harbinger Publications, 1994), p. 2.

7. *Ibid.*, p. 156.

8. Kipnis, *Knights Without Armor*, pp. 15–18.

9. James B. Nelson, *The Intimate Connection: Male Sexuality and Masculine Spirituality* (Philadelphia: Westminster Press, 1988).

10. Keen, *Fire in the Belly*, p. 110.

11. Diamond, *The Warrior's Journey Home*, p. 17.

12. *Ibid.*, p. 55.

13. *Ibid.*, p. 74.

14. *Ibid.*, p. 75.

15. *Ibid.*, pp. 78–81.

16. *Ibid.*, pp. 28–31.

17. *Ibid.*, p. 107.

18. Interview with Bill Moyers, *A Gathering of Men with Robert Bly*, video (New York: Public Television Corporation, 1990).

19. Robert Bly, *Iron John: A Book About Men* (New York: Vintage Books/Random House, 1992), p. 94.

20. Guy Corneau, *Absent Fathers, Lost Sons: The Search for a New Masculine Identity* (Boston: Shambhala Publications, 1991), p. 11.

21. *Ibid.*, pp. 12–13.

22. *Ibid.*, p. 13.

23. *Ibid.*, pp. 17–18.

24. *Ibid.*, pp. 18–19.

25. *Ibid.*, p. 19.

26. *Ibid.*, pp. 19–21.

27. Patrick J. Arnold, *Wildmen, Warriors and Kings: Masculine Spirituality and the Bible* (New York: Crossroad, 1992), p. 96.

28. *Ibid.*, p. 37.

29. "The Kronos in each of us has the tendency to 'eat' our children, to devour the younger generation in order to maintain our own hard-fought security." Judy, *Healing the Male Soul*, p. 139.

30. *Ibid.*, p. 200.

31. Nelson, *The Intimate Connection*, pp. 116–118.

32. *Ibid.*, p. 116.

33. Steven Hill, *A Man Thinks About Pornography: Beauty, Images, and Totalitarianism* (Bellingham: Tow Hill, 1988), p. 117.

34. Don Sabo, "The Myth of the Sexual Athlete," in *Men and Intimacy: Personal Accounts Exploring the Dilemmas of Modern Male Sexuality*, edited by Franklin Abbot (Freedom: Crossing Press, 1990), pp. 16–20.

35. Keen, *Fire in the Belly*, p. 75.

36. Diamond, *The Warrior's Journey Home*, pp. 80–81.

37. The number of authors who condemn circumcision as a warrant-less attack are profound. See *ibid.*, pp. 139–149, for a helpful discussion in this regard.

38. Philip Culbertson, *The New Adam: The Future of Male Spirituality* (Minneapolis: Augsburg Fortress Press, 1992), pp. 23–25.

39. Daniel A. Helminiak, *What the Bible Really Says About Homosexuality* (San Francisco: Alamo Square Press, 1994), p. 12.

40. *Ibid.*, pp. 12–13.

41. John J. McNeill, *The Church and the Homosexual* (Kansas City: Sheed Andrews and McMeel, 1976), p. 121.

42. Nelson, *The Intimate Connection*, p. 116.

43. *Ibid.*, p. 13.

44. Bly, *Iron John*, p. 86.

45. Culbertson, *The New Adam*, p. 113.

46. Arnold, *Wildmen, Warriors and Kings*, p. 45.

47. Johnson, *He: Understanding Masculine Psychology*, Revised Edition (New York: Harper and Row Publishers, 1989), p. 36.

48. Robert Johnson, *Lying with the Heavenly Woman* (San Francisco: HarperCollins, 1994), pp. 19–32.

49. Kipnis, *Knights Without Armor*, pp. vii–x.

50. Keen, *Fire in the Belly*, pp. 128–149.

51. Judy, *Healing the Male Soul*, pp. 156–181.

52. Culbertson, *The New Adam*, pp. 23–25.

53. Diamond, *The Warrior's Journey Home*, pp. 55–69.

54. *Ibid.*, p. 20.

55. *Ibid.*, pp. 100–106.

56. *Ibid.*, pp. 107–116.

57. *Ibid.*, pp. 118–127.

58. *Ibid.*, p. 22.

59. *Ibid.*, pp. 137–164.

60. *Ibid.*, pp. 166–170.

61. *Ibid.*, pp. 171–180.

62. *Ibid.*, pp. 190–200.

63. *Ibid.*, pp. 235–240.

64. Judy, *Healing the Male Soul*, p. 114.

65. *Ibid.*, p. 118.

66. *Ibid.*, p. 119.

67. Matthew Fox, *Original Blessing: A Primer in Creation Spirituality* (Santa Fe: Bear & Co., 1980).

68. Judy, *Healing the Male Soul*, p. 133.

69. *Ibid.*, pp. 125–126.

70. *Ibid.*, p. 169.

71. Diamond, *The Warrior's Journey Home*, pp. 111–113.

72. Carl Koch and Joyce Heil, *Created in God's Image: Meditating on Our Body* (Winona: St. Mary's Press, 1991). See pp. 46–50 for a prayer/meditation exercise designed to heal a man's body shame.

73. Nelson, *The Intimate Connection*, p. 116.

74. Arnold, *Wildmen, Warriors and Kings*, p. 49.

75. Johnson, *He: Understanding Masculine Psychology*, pp. 34–37.

76. "In our age, the time has come to embrace all opposites and to cherish our passions. It is a time to embrace our full natures, physical as well as spiritual, and in this new embrace with the earth to profoundly embrace woman, as well." Judy, *Healing the Male Soul*, p. 158.

77. *Ibid.*, p. 179.

Chapter 5

1. Aaron Kipnis, *Knights Without Armor: A Practical Guide for Men in Quest of the Masculine Soul* (New York: Tarcher/Pedigree Books, 1991), p. 19.

2. *Ibid.*, p. 19.

3. Patrick Arnold, *Wildmen, Warriors and Kings: Masculine Spirituality and the Bible* (New York: Crossroad, 1992), p. 136.

4. Robert Bly, *Iron John: A Book About Men* (New York: Vintage Books/Random House, 1992), p. 33.

5. Jed Diamond, *The Warrior's Journey Home: Healing Men, Healing the Planet* (Oakland: New Harbinger Publications, 1994), p. 21.

6. Kipnis, *Knights Without Armor,* pp. 20–21.

7. Diamond, *The Warrior's Journey Home* pp. 108–109.

8. Sam Keen, *Fire in the Belly: On Being a Man* (New York: Bantam Books, 1991), p. 234.

9. *Ibid.*, p. 229.

10. *Ibid.*, p. 234.

11. Bill Kauth, *A Circle of Men: The Original Manual for Men's Support Groups* (New York: St. Martin's Press, 1992), p. 5.

12. Arnold, *Wildmen, Warriors and Kings*, p. 136.

13. Kipnis, *Knights Without Armor*, p. 232.

14. *Ibid.*, p. 80.

15. *Ibid.*, p. 230.

16. Jerome S. Bernstein, "Introduction," in *To Be a Man: In Search of the Deep Masculine*, edited by Keith Thompson (Los Angeles: Jeremy P. Tarcher, Inc., 1991), p. 36.

17. *Ibid.*, p. 112.

18. *Ibid.*, p. 58.

19. *Ibid.*, p. 201.

20. *Ibid.*, p. 234.

21. Kauth, *A Circle of Men.* See pp. 98–99 for insights on how men need to be taught to be intimate with other men.

22. Philip Culbertson, *The New Adam: The Future of Male Spirituality* (Minneapolis: Augsburg Fortress Press, 1992), pp. 130–131.

23. Kauth, *A Circle of Men*, pp. 72–73.

24. Kipnis, *Knights Without Armor*, pp. vii-x.

25. Keen, *Fire in the Belly*, pp. 235–242.

26. Diamond, *The Warrior's Journey Home*, p. 110.

27. Richard Rohr and Joseph Martos, *The Wildman's Journey: Reflections on Male Spirituality* (Cincinnati: St. Anthony Messenger Press, 1992), p. 179.

28. *Ibid.*

29. Diamond, *The Warrior's Journey Home*, p. 113.

30. Kipnis, *Knights Without Armor*, p. 205.

31. Bly, *Iron John*, p. 99.

32. *Ibid.*, p. 100.

33. Rohr and Martos, *The Wildman's Journey*, pp. 209–212.

34. *Ibid.*, p. 184.

35. Kipnis, *Knights Without Armor*, p. 159.

36. *Ibid.*

37. *Ibid.*, p. 161.

38. Diamond, *The Warrior's Journey Home*, p. 199.

39. Kipnis, *Knights Without Armor*, p. 162.

40. Arnold, *Wildmen, Warriors and Kings*, p. 167.

41. *Ibid.*

42. Rohr and Martos, *The Wildman's Journey*, pp. 205–206.

43. Arnold, *Wildmen, Warriors and Kings*, p. 175.

44. Kipnis, *Knights Without Armor*, pp. 177–178.

45. *Ibid.*, p. 183.

46. *Ibid.*, p. 187.

47. *Ibid.*, p. 183.

48. Keen, *Fire in the Belly*, pp. 22–23.

49. *Ibid.*, pp. 174–175.

50. Culbertson, *The New Adam*, p. 75.

51. Bly, *Iron John*, p. 32.

52. *Ibid.*, p. 91.

53. *Ibid.*

54. *Ibid.*, p. 90.

55. *Ibid.*, p. 95.

56. Keen, *Fire in the Belly*, p. 28.

57. Diamond, *The Warrior's Journey Home*, pp. 105–106.

58. Kipnis, *Knights Without Armor*, p. 164.

59. See Robert Johnson, *Lying with the Heavenly Woman*, pp. 45–47, for a helpful review of a man's need to psychologically discriminate from women.

60. Culbertson, *The New Adam*, p. 5.

61. Keen, *Fire in the Belly*, p. 28.

62. Kipnis, *Knights Without Armor*, p. 163.

63. Bly, *Iron John*, p. 32.

64. Robert Moore and Douglas Gillette, *King, Warrior, Magician, Lover: Rediscovering the Archetypes of the Mature Masculine* (New York: HarperCollins Publishers, 1990), p. 3.

65. Arnold, *Wildmen, Warriors and Kings*, p. 42.

66. Bly, *Iron John*, p. 32.

67. Rohr and Martos, *The Wildman's Journey*, p. 50.

68. Moore and Gillette, *King, Warrior, Magician, Lover*, p. 5.

69. *Ibid.*, pp. 5–7.

70. Arnold, *Wildmen, Warriors and Kings*, p. 42.

71. *Ibid.*, pp. 42–43.

72. *Ibid.*, p. 43.

73. Rohr and Martos, *The Wildman's Journey*, pp. 49–50.

74. Arnold, *Wildmen, Warriors and Kings*, p. 73.

75. *Ibid.*, pp. 74–75.

76. *Ibid.*, p. 74.

77. *Ibid.*, p. 50.

78. Keen, *Fire in the Belly*, p. 245.

79. Kipnis, *Knights Without Armor*, p. 281.

80. Dwight H. Judy, *Healing the Male Soul: Christianity and the Mythic Journey* (New York: Crossroad, 1992), p. 180.

81. Rohr and Martos, *The Wildman's Journey*, p. 225.

82. Arnold, *Wildmen, Warriors and Kings*, p. 50.

83. Kauth, *A Circle of Men*, p. 129.

Other Books in This Series

Other Books in This Series

What are they saying about Scripture and Ethics?
(Revised and Expanded Ed.)
by William C. Spohn
What are they saying about Unbelief?
by Michael Paul Gallagher, S.J.